Machu P[icchu]

The Ultimate Guide B[ook to]
Machu Picchu and its Hidden Places.

By Anton Swanepoel

Amazon Kindle ASIN: B00A2D1LN0
Print ISBN- 1480192279
Print ISBN-13: 978-1480192270
Smashwords ISBN: 9781311586537

All images are property of Anton Swanepoel, except where otherwise stated.

Anton Swanepoel

http://antonswanepoelbooks.com/
http://antonswanepoelbooks.com/blog/
http://www.facebook.com/AuthorAntonSwanepoel
https://twitter.com/Author_Anton

Follow this link: http://antonswanepoelbooks.com/subscribe.php to get updates on new book releases.

Introduction

Mystical Machu Picchu is on the bucket list of many people, and rightly so, for it is a stunning place offering more than one might realize. For some, Machu Picchu is a place to grow spiritually, while for others it is a place to admire the architecture and the magnificent feat of building a city on top of a mountain. Regardless of your reasons almost all agree that Machu Picchu has a majestic lure, a magnetism that cannot be explained. There is certainly more to Machu Picchu than meets the eye.

Although this book does cover some of Machu Picchu's history, as well as new findings and analysis of soil and bone samples from graves to determine what Machu Picchu was really used for and what the people ate at Machu Picchu, it is not the aim of this book to give a detailed archeological explanation of the ruins and the history of the Inca Empire. The focus of this book is to show you what to expect on your visit, as well as give you interesting facts and theories about Machu Picchu without getting too technical. Information is given in relevant chunks, alongside the corresponding picture of the objects being described, allowing the reader to easily find the information being sought for what is in front of them at the time of their Machu Picchu visit.

A big decision for many people is exactly how much time to spend at Machu Picchu. Many visit the ruins for only a few hours as part of a tour package. Although it is comfortable having someone plan the trip for you, it is expensive and in many cases you will be rushed through the ruins and miss stunning attractions such as Mountain Huayna Picchu and Mountain Machu Picchu, not to mention the Inca Bridge, Lunar Temple and Grand Cavern or Hot Springs. Contained in the book is over 200 pictures, showing you how Machu Picchu actually looks, as well as information and links to help you easily plan your own trip for a fraction of the price of a tour package.

Welcome to Sacred Machu Picchu -- it will change your live forever.

Disclaimer

All the services, hotels, websites, products and companies mentioned in this book are from my own experience and use or what I deem to be helpful.

I do not promote any products or services for any company, nor do I receive any gains from any company to promote them. Further, I take no responsibility for anyone using any services or companies suggested in this book.

The companies mentioned have the right to change their products, services as well as prices without prior notice.

The ruins at Machu Picchu is covered in a walk-through style, taking a route that will take you to all the major attractions, with pictures of each. This route will take around three hours to complete. All other attractions such as both mountains, are covered separately, with time to visit given for each attraction.

Table of Contents

Chapter 1: The Boring Stuff

This chapter covers important items that are often overlooked and can potentially halt your vacation or make it a miserable experience.

Visas and Vaccinations

Most tourists do not need a visa for staying up to 183 days in Peru. Make sure you have a visa for all transiting places and Peru if you need it. Good websites to check are:
http://www.antonswanepoelbooks.com/peru_visa_information.php
http://www.limaeasy.com/peru-info/peruvian-visa
http://www.embaperu.org.au/embassy/visas.html

Exit Fee

Peru, like many other countries, charges an exit or departure tax. With most airlines the tax is already included in your ticket price. If the tax is not included then you can pay it at the airport after checking in. There is normally a small kiosk with a sign saying airport or departure tax. The tax is around US $5-10. Note, domestic flights from Juliaca and Iquitos may charge an addition fee of approximately US $5.

Checking the Weather

It is not only important to check the weather before you go, but also while you are there. There are a number of websites that will give you updates, here are a few:
http://www.antonswanepoelbooks.com/machu_picchu.php
http://www.accuweather.com/en/pe/machu-picchu/262837/weather-forecast/262837
http://www.worldweatheronline.com/v2/weather.aspx?q=MFT
http://www.zoover.co.uk/peru/peru/machu-picchu/weather
http://www.intermeteo.com/south_america/peru/machu_picchu/

What Time of the Year to Go

Machu Picchu, being at a high altitude, has a temperature of between 10 and 30 degrees Celsius (50 to 86 degrees Fahrenheit).

There are basically two seasons; a dry season, and a rainy season running from November to April, with January and February being the wettest months.

However, Machu Picchu is almost surrounded by fog on many days and short showers can be expected at any time, especially early in the morning.

July to August is the high season when most of the tourists go, as the nights are cooler with the days normally being dry. Personally, I went in September and found the temperature to be cool, with not too many tourists, especially before 11am. Most of the days were dry, with a few only having a slight drizzle early in the morning that cleared by 10am.

To avoid crowds, try to plan your trip when schools are not closed and universities do not have breaks. Also, go early in the morning and catch the first bus and stay in the town Machu Picchu Pueblo (Aguas Calientes, meaning hot springs, and was the old name of the town due to the hot springs found in the town). Many tourists stay in either Ollantaytambo or Cusco and take the early train and bus, thus they will arrive around 10am and leave around 2pm, making these times the busiest at the ruins and the bus stop.

How Much Will It Cost?

What your trip will cost is highly dependent on how cheap you want to travel and what comforts you want when you get to your destination. Make no mistake, Peru, and especially Machu Picchu, is a tourist attraction, and prices will be more than what you might expect in many other places.

You can save money by looking for cheaper restaurants, haggle a bit over prices of stuff sold in local markets, and take cheaper accommodations. At restaurants, ask if they automatically add a tip or service charge. It is frustrating when you get a meal for 10 Sol that is ok but then get slapped with a 5 Sol service charge, whereas you could have had a far better meal at another location for the same price, thus the price on the menu is not always what you pay.

There are a number of ATM machines in Machu Picchu. However, almost all places accept Visa and Master cards, and all accept US dollars. A few places will do money exchange to local Sol. Expect around 2.5 to 2.6 conversion, with the norm being 2.5 Sol per 1 US dollar. Note, make sure you check the change, as some shops 'accidentally' give you the wrong change.

The basic cost for one day will be:
-Entry to ruins US $72 (Through online service) (+-$50 at official site)
-Entry to Museum, add US $10 to entry price
-Entry to Mountain Huayna Picchu, add US $10 to entry price
-Entry to Mountain Machu Picchu, add US $10 to entry price
-Guide at ruins, around US $20
-Bus to ruins, return US $17
-Train from Ollantaytambo, return US $110, Inca Railway (Executive service)
-Taxi from Cusco to Ollantaytambo, around US $35 to $60 one way, private

Google Search Reverting To Spanish
When you travel, Google and many of the websites automatically display in the local language. This can be annoying, especially if you are not fluent in the local language and are trying to find your online booking in a hurry. To stop this from happening to Google, try typing in *www.google.com/ncr*

Safe Zones
Peru, including Machu Picchu, is subject to earthquakes, mudslides, and other natural disasters such as rocks and boulders sliding down a mountain and blocking a road, including possibly injuring people. Zones that are marked with signs as 'Safe Zones' are zones that should be safe in case of an earthquake or other natural disasters.

Chapter 2: How Much Time?

This is probably one of the most difficult decisions to make, just exactly how many days to spend where. Sadly, many people do not give adequate time for themselves to truly discover the ruins. This is due to a variety of reasons including the following: not enough holiday time booked, spending too much time in Cusco or Lima, not knowing there is so much to see, miscalculating the time needed to climb the mountains or walk the ruins, booking a guided trip that will rush you through, and a host of other reasons.

In this section times to the major destinations are listed to give you an idea of how much time to plan for your visit.

Cutting to the chase – to see all of Machu Picchu's wonders you are going to need at least two full days if you are a fit person, and about three to four days if you need some rest. Although it is possible to see both mountains on the same day, you would need to be super fit to manage it. This will leave you little time to see anything else, as well you will need to purchase two entry tickets to the ruins for the same day, as entries to the mountains are add-on to your entry ticket.

Only Machu Picchu
Ok, if you are only interested in seeing the ruins and nothing else, then you can do a gentle walk through the ruins in about three hours. This allows plenty of time to stop and take photos and rest. Allow about one hour for the bus ride up and one hour down (30 minutes waiting time for the bus either way, ride itself is about 30 minutes). This is what you will get on a one day tour package (three hours at the ruins).

Inca Bridge
The Inca Bridge is approximately a 20 minute hike one way. The hike compared to any other hike, such as Inti Punku or climbing the mountains, is easy.

Allow yourself an hour to 1½ hours to do this hike in total, depending on your fitness level, with time spent at the gate. Note, you have to sign in and out at a small hut by the entrance. Sometimes you spend much of your time waiting for people to sign the book, as the bridge is popular.

Intipunku (The Door of the Sun)

Inti Punku (also called 'The Door of the Sun' or 'Gateway of The Sun') is roughly an hour to 1½ hours hike one way, thus allow yourself three hours for this hike. Compared to the climb up the mountain it is relatively easy, but it is a long distance to walk. If you walk very fast, something I do not recommend due to loose rocks, you can do it in two hours return. However, the scenery on this trail is part of the hike itself and spending time sitting at the gate should be included. Note, some people list this as a 45 minute hike, which is possible on the return if you are fit, but unrealistic for the walk up for most people.

Mountain Huayna Picchu (Wayna Picchu)

Mountain Huayna Picchu is also known as Wayna Picchu, meaning 'Young Peak' in Quechua. The climb to the mountain is around 45 minutes to one hour, with the same amount for the return. Thus allow yourself two hours to do this climb and enjoy some time at the top and along the way.

The climb is sometimes steep but railings and cables are provided to assist you. For the time spent to get to the top, this is well worth the climb. Note that this is the more popular of the two mountains, and 400 people are allowed to climb the mountain a day in two groups; group one starting at 7am and group two starting at 9am. The top of the mountain is very small and does not allow for many people to sit there, so go earlier if you want to avoid the crowds.

Lunar Temple and Grand Cavern

Visiting the Lunar Temple and Grand Cavern is highly recommended and should be added to your climb of Mountain Huayna Picchu, if you have the time.

The total round trip is around two to three hours extra for the climb up the mountain, depending on your fitness level. Doing both should take you around four or so hours.

To get to the caves one can either climb the mountain and return on the alternative path that passes the Temple, or take the path to the Temple at the split half-way up to Mountain Huayna Picchu before you reach the top (see the section on Lunar Temple later in the book for photos). The Lunar Temple and Grand Cavern are close together, with the Temple being a little higher up the mountain. See section on Lunar Temple for more details.

Mountain Machu Picchu

It is interesting to see how many people misjudge this mountain. The climb to the top is roughly 1½ to two hours, with about the same time to get back. Thus allow yourself about four hours or so for this climb. Only 300 people are allowed per day.

This mountain is higher than the rest, and you will most probably experience some altitude sickness signs, so take it easy. The climb is definitely well worth it. Note, this climb can be steep at points with small steps, loose rocks and no railings. It is a longer, harder and more dangerous climb than Mountain Huayna Picchu, however the views are far better. I suggest to do both mountains if you can, but not on the same day. ☺

Museum and Botanical Garden

The museum is at the bottom of the town Machu Picchu Pueblo and not close to the ruins or the town itself for that matter (around 20 to 30 minute stroll down from the town). Note, taking photos is not allowed in the museum. There is a botanical garden that you can also visit at the museum.

Entry tickets can be purchased as an add-on to your ticket to the ruins, or you can buy a ticket at the museum entrance. Allow two hours for the return hike to see both the museum and the garden. Alternatively, you can politely ask the bus driver to drop you at the museum on your way back from the ruins.

Hot Springs

The hot springs are a 15 to 20 minute slow walk up from the main steel bridge, see photos later in the book. The springs are open from 8am to 5pm, thus the time needed here depends entirely upon you. There is a bar and small restaurant at the springs, however, you can exit and return later at will on the same day. Tickets are bought at the gate of the springs.

Machu Picchu Pueblo

This is an expanding town and development and construction is ongoing all over. Some construction is repairs from recent floods, however, it does not comfort you to know that when you are trying to rest (can go on in places until 11pm at night, but rarely and is only temporary).

The town has a craft market that can hold its own to many other craft markets in Peru, with a variety of small shops selling all manner of souvenirs, and a number of restaurants.

Although the town can be walked through from side to side in about two hours, I would give it at least half a day to a full day to really experience the town. Note, this town is not like Ollantaytambo that has a historical feel to it, but a town built for tourists. Thus, if you want to shop for local Inca craft, there are plenty here.

Lima

Lima is by the ocean and has stunning beaches. The town itself is modern and there are plenty of shops to choose from. If you want to have a quick browse around and see the main plaza, then half a day to a day should do. However, if you want to do some tanning on the beach and see the nightlife, then the amount of time you need for Lima is totally up to you. For more information on Lima, see *http://www.limaeasy.com/index.php*

Cusco

After Lima, Cusco is normally the second stop for most people.

Many stay a few days in Cusco, acclimatizing to the high altitude and visiting some of the ruins in Cusco. Note however, that Cusco is higher up than Machu Picchu, and you can actually first go to Machu Picchu, adjust to the altitude there and then on your return visit Cusco.

Cusco was the capital city of the Inca Empire, and one can see the different stages the city went through as different rulers had control of the city and empire. Cusco is currently the oldest inhabited city in the Americas and has some great monasteries and cathedrals that are worth seeing.

For shopping, nightlife and good dining, many people head to the 'Plaza de Armas', and a day spent here is well worth it. If you stay in Cusco, try to get the train directly from Cusco to Machu Picchu, else a taxi to Ollantaytambo is a good option.

Urubamba (Sacred Valley)
The town of Urubamba is located near the Urubamba River under the snow-capped mountain of Chicón, and is the largest town in the Sacred Valley. It is about one hour from Cusco. The town, like Ollantaytambo, has a historic feel to it and has very good dining.

Ollantaytambo
This town has some historic feel to it, and very interesting ruins right in the town. Entry tickets to the ruins are sold at the gates, however note that at time of writing it was 172 Sols, more than an entry ticket for Machu Picchu. The town has a few shops and plaza, including some nice restaurants.

Since the town is the main departure point for many of the trains, it is easy to plan to stay a few hours or even a night here. You should be able to walk through the town and the ruins in half a day to possibly a full day to enjoy a relaxed time here.

Chapter 3: What to Take With

This chapter covers more everyday things rather than what to bring if you are doing the Inca trail. It is not an all-exclusive list, but a basic one to help you remember the small things that can make your trip go smoother.

First, note that the only luggage you can take on the trains has to be in a bag or suitcase the same size that will fit in an airline carry-on, unless you take the backpacker train.

In many cases this should be sufficient unless you stay more than two days or have a need to bring everything you own with on your trip. Thus, arrange for your main luggage to be stored at a hotel if you stayed in Cusco or Lima and have large suitcases.

Washing

There is no need to bring more than three days of clothing, as most hotels do washing in both Machu Picchu Pueblo and Ollantaytambo. Cost is around 10 to 12 Sols per kilogram (2 pounds) of washing. There are also a number of independent places that will do your washing for you and many deliver to your room. Service is good; I had delicate clothes and found no problems with the service, except that it can be sometimes slow. Thus allow a day for washing.

Mosquito Repellent

If you are going to stay in the campsite or do the trail, take mosquito repellent. You can tell who did the trail, as they are riddled with insect bites. There are plenty of shops selling mosquito repellant in both Machu Picchu Pueblo and Ollantaytambo, so no need to take loads with you on the airplane.

Batteries

If your camera or flashlight takes normal AAA, AA, C or D-cell batteries, then those are easy to obtain in the towns, at relatively higher prices.

If you are doing the Inca trail, then you can purchase batteries in Cusco before the start of your trip.

Flashlight

There are really only two reasons to bring a flashlight. First, if you are doing the Inca trail, in which case I would suggest a very good headlamp of at least 100 to 200 Lumens and preferably with an external battery pack. Second, if you are planning to hike up the mountain to the entry gate and not take the bus, and wish to be there when the gate opens. In this case, I also recommend a headlamp, however, a smaller 50 to 100 Lumens will do. Note that in some months, like September, the sun rises at about 5:45am before the gate opens at 6am. Furthermore, note that the sun rises behind the mountain so it will be around 9 to 10am before direct sunlight hits Machu Picchu, not to mention that about 60% of the time Machu Picchu is covered in mist (fog) early in the morning.

Laptop

If you plan to download photos from your camera or to Skype call, but do not want to carry a laptop just for those purposes, then there is hope. There are plenty of places in Machu Picchu that offer Internet services and have computers for use. Many also offer the service to download your photos and burn them to a compact disc for you. Most restaurants and hotels in Peru offer free Internet. The connection is normally good enough to do Skype calls on your smart phone.

Toiletries

Machu Picchu Pueblo is a town larger than expected, and everyday items like shampoo, soap, shaving cream and even baby powder and milk or diapers are obtainable in the town. Thus, if you are stuck with having to leave something, these items can be bought in the town.

Warm Clothing

How much warm clothing to take will entirely depend on where you are coming from and the time of year you go.

In September, when I went, the temperature was in the high 70's Fahrenheit (mid 20's Celsius). The morning air was cool, yet within 10 minutes of climbing a mountain I was sweating in only my T-shirt. I found the night air to be a little cool walking around, but you can pick up a lovely jersey made from Lama hair for a song that will keep you warm and serve as a souvenir. I suggest taking a fleece jacket as it is very warm for its weight.

If you are doing the trek, then you are going to need some warm, waterproof clothes in most cases. Ask your booking agent or guide what to bring for the time of year you are going. Do include warm socks and long pants.

Comfortable Shoes

This is a must, irrespective if you are only visiting the ruins or hiking the trail or want to climb the mountains. The ruins themselves have over 3000 steps with multiple paths leading up and down, thus it is best to bring hiking shoes or trail shoes. Although sneakers or trainers can be used when climbing the mountains, the risk of stepping wrong and hurting an ankle is high.

Cell Phone

Interestingly there is cell reception at both the ruins and in Machu Picchu Pueblo. You are confronted by a sales person trying to rent you a cell phone when leaving the airports in most places. However, you can purchase a local SIM card if your phone is unlocked.

Camera

I was surprised by two things on my trip. One, just how many people use their camera on their cell phones these days, and two, that they sell digital cameras and camera memory cards in the town Machu Picchu Pueblo. However, do note that it will cost you more than getting it on Amazon or e-bay. However, if you forget your camera and only remember it when you get to Machu Picchu Pueblo, and have the money, then you can still have photos of your trip.

Plug Adapter

The power in Peru is 220 volts at around 50 hertz. The plug sockets in all the hotels and places I checked, take both the US standard flat two prong and the European (such as South Africa) round two-prong. Hardly any plug sockets take three prongs.

Antibiotics and Imodium

Yup, you can get sick, and I did around day three when drinking local water. I got a soft drink that was made from local water (machine mix and not bottled) and got sick the next morning. There are a number of drug stores (chemists) in the town, and you only need to point to your stomach for them to get the message. I was handed antibiotics and Imodium without questions and was ready to continue exploring the next day.

Hat, Sun Block and Shades

I highly recommend you bring a hat, unless you want to get one at Machu Picchu Pueblo itself. I paid 10 Sol for a Camo hat (same ones you see in movies that the Navy Seals use). Also remember to get some sun block or sunscreen.

Gloves

You can purchase Lama hair gloves in the town if it is cold, however, I do recommend bringing cheap garden or working gloves to protect your hands while you climb. Many of the steps on the big mountain are steep, and you almost do it on all fours, including the guide rails on the smaller mountain being covered in rust. No need to go all out with thick gloves, simple material garden or mechanic gloves are perfect, giving good cut protection while not compromising feel and dexterity. There are no real thorns to worry about at Machu Picchu.

Personal Medication

If you need an Asthma pump or insulin or any other medication, take it with you.

The air is dry and dusty at the ruins, and the high altitude can cause an attack. From the ruins, it is a 30 minute bus ride. Sometimes you may wait for an hour to get on a bus (around 12 to 3pm) just to get to the town Machu Picchu Pueblo, and if your medicine is a prescription it may not be available there. That will take you another four or more hours to Cusco if you are lucky enough to get on a train when you get to the town.

There is a helipad in Machu Picchu and a stretcher with medical support at the ruins. Thus, in real emergencies, you can be airlifted directly from the ruins or the town, but I suspect at a premium price, so make sure you take your camera with as the view would be spectacular from a helicopter over the ruins (that is if you are conscious at the time ☺).

Rain Jacket or Poncho

It can rain a lot at the ruins, depending on the month you go. When I went in September it only rained one morning for about two hours while I was at the ruins. I bought a North Face summit series jacket for US $60 in Machu Picchu. Almost every shop sells lightweight ponchos. If you are going in the rainy season, especially if you do the Inca trail, then you are advised to take proper rain gear. It can get very cold when the mountain air blows in, especially if you are wet.

Passport

Yes, we know you need to have your passport to fly international and enter Peru, but you need your passport to enter the ruins at Machu Picchu, as well as get your train tickets. So do not leave it in your hotel room, especially if your hotel room is in Cusco with the rest of your luggage. You need six months still remaining on your passport after your planned date of entry into Peru.

Water

Do remember to take plenty of water with you. I recommend at least two liters of water per person if you are there for half a day, and three to four liters per person if you are climbing the mountain and staying a full day.

You can exit the ruins and purchase some more water outside if you do not want to take all of it up the mountain; however, it is a little bit more expensive at the ruins.

Altitude Sickness

Machu Picchu is at higher altitudes, and climbing the mountains, especially Mountain Machu Picchu, will probably cause you to experience altitude sickness symptoms.

Due to the air pressure being less at altitude, the amount of oxygen to your body is less. This causes a state of hypoxia with symptoms such as headache, loss of appetite, difficulty breathing, vomiting, reduced fitness ability (feeling weak), dizziness (can be dangerous on a mountain path), confusion and trouble sleeping. It is currently thought that your fitness level and being male or female play no role in whether you get altitude sickness.

Symptoms can range from only mild to totally incapacitating and life threatening. In some cases, symptoms may only be felt a day after arriving at altitude. However, onset can be fast, especially if you fly to altitude.

Rest often and drink plenty of water. You can drink some of the local Coca tea (also called mate de coca) or eat some of the Coca sweets. Note, Coca leaf that is used to make Coca tea contains alkaloids, which when extracted is used in the production of cocaine. One gram of Coca leaf (the typical contents of a tea bag) contains ±4.2 mg of organic coca alkaloid, and a typical line of cocaine contains between 20 and 30 mg - the consumption of one cup of Coca tea can cause a positive result on a drug test for cocaine. Also note that Coca tea, although legal in Peru, Bolivia, Colombia, and Ecuador, is illegal in the United States. While Coca tea is often recommended for travelers to prevent altitude sickness, its actual effectiveness has never been systematically studied.

You can also opt for a medical alternative from a local chemist. Personally, I opted for bodybuilding pills that are designed to increase the amount of oxygen to the muscles. This worked well for me.

For more information on altitude sickness see International Society for Mountain Medicine (*http://www.ismmed.org./*) and *http://www.traveldoctor.co.uk/altitude.htm.*

Energy Drinks

You do sweat a lot at higher altitudes and use a lot of energy, thus you lose a large amount of electrolytes. Drinking sports drinks or eating electrolyte gels will help you recover some of the lost minerals.

Snacks

Do remember to take some snacks along. As a rule, you are not supposed to take any food into the ruins. However, bags are not normally checked and a small amount of snacks is okay to take in.

Some power bars, crackers, bananas and apples will be a good option. If you have time to visit Machu Picchu Pueblo, then most of the shops sell health and protein bars. You can also make your own sandwiches if you like. Some of the hotels give a day pack for the ruins, check with the Reception.

Note, food like cereal bars and salty snack, such as crackers, will need water to be digested and cause you to drink more water, so plan for it. For a morning out, you should not need more than four or so bars per person and a banana or an apple.

Chapter 4: Getting To Machu Picchu

There are a number of different options in getting to the ruins, from cheap backpacking and hitchhiking to private taxis. This chapter deals with the more commonly used methods of getting to Machu Picchu and the towns you can stay in.

Lima

Of all the entry points into Peru, Lima is the major one and will, in most instances, be your first port of call when entering Peru. There are daily flights from many major countries, with USA (Miami airport) being one of the best options. Lima, in reality, is not an option to stay in to reach the ruins the same day, while having any meaningful time there. Even if you get it right and get an early flight in the morning to Cusco, it is still three hours from Cusco to Machu Picchu Pueblo, excluding waiting for a taxi or train, and another 30 minutes to the entry gate if you manage to walk directly off the train and onto a bus to the ruins.

Note, your baggage does not get automatically transferred to the following flight even if you have a ticket all the way to Cusco. You will have to collect any luggage yourself in Lima if you are flying to Cusco or any other airport. Allow yourself at least two hours between flights. It may be possible to clear customs earlier, but it will remove some stress if you are not worried about missing your next flight. If you plan on getting a bite to eat and doing some shopping, then around four hours is recommended.

Cusco

Locals believe that Cusco is the navel of the universe, and have been farming in Cusco since the 12th century. It is from Cusco, that approximately 100,000 Incas, ruled up to 12 million subjects. The empire at its peak in 1532, stretched from Columbia to Chile, over 2000 miles (3200 kilometers). At this time, the empire was around 100 years old, and about to collapse due to three factors.

Anton Swanepoel

First, smallpox brought to South America by the Spanish, spread from Mexico to the Andres, and killed an estimated 50% or more of the population. Second, the Inca emperor died and his two sons engaged in a bloody fight for the crown, splitting the empire in two. Lastly, the Spanish under the command of Francisco Pizarro, arrived in Peru, determined to subjugate the locals and plunder their treasures.

For most visitors to Peru, Cusco is the second stop on their way to Machu Picchu. Many tourists acclimatize in Cusco to the altitude. However, Cusco is actually higher than Machu Picchu. Many tour companies lead people to believe that it is better to stay in Cusco for a few days before going to Machu Picchu. However, this is just to get them to shop where they want them to. If you have no inclination to see Cusco, it is better to head directly to Machu Picchu.

The fastest way from Lima to Cusco, it to take an inland flight. Try to book a through-ticket from your original departure to Cusco and return. Try to keep to the same airline for all legs of the trip. If you booked a through-ticket, and a flight is delayed, then you do not need to fork out the money for missing your next flight. It is the airline's problem. Cusco airport itself is very small. There is a small food court on the second floor, with basically three eating places. Note that the departure's area has no eating places and is basically just a big open space with chairs. If you are planning to get something to eat, do not go through security until you are ready to board the plane. However, that said, seating can quickly become limited at the food court, and if you are planning on taking a nap, there is more seating in the departure's area.

A bus from Lima to Cusco, will save you between US $70 to $100, depending on the service level. However, you will lose a lot of time if you are on a tight schedule. There are a number of tour operators; here is a website that provides a service similar to Expedia. *http://www.go2peru.com/ecs_ing.htm*

To get from Cusco to Machu Picchu, you have three main options. You can hike the Inca trail, but I do not recommend it. The trail is long and hard, and you do not see much more than what you would see hiking the two mountains at Machu Picchu.

You can alternatively take a train from Cusco directly to Machu Picchu Pueblo (town below Machu Picchu Ruins), with Peru Rail. The services provided are the famous 'Hiram Bingham Deluxe Train', 'Vistadome' and the 'Expedition Class'.

See *www.perurail.com* for more information. Note that the train does not depart from Cusco itself, but from Poroy Station, that is 20 minutes from Cusco city, thus you will need to get a taxi to the station from the airport or your hotel.

Lastly, you can take a taxi or bus from Cusco to Ollantaytambo. This is the most popular and cheaper option. Taxis are available right outside Cusco airport arrival's terminal. When exiting the terminal building, you will see a number of taxis to your left. You can elect to obtain a taxi yourself, or make use of the service provided by the kiosk just before you exit the departure's area. Note, you will, in many cases, be able to get a far better deal if you obtain a taxi yourself, however, if you are unsure or do not want to haggle with prices – use the service provided by the kiosk. You can also purchase bus tickets to Ollantaytambo at the kiosk. I paid US $60 for a private taxi from Cusco using the kiosk, and paid half that for a private taxi on my return by bypassing the kiosk. Travel time from Cusco airport to Ollantaytambo is about two hours.

If you elect to use a bus to Ollantaytambo, then you will have to wait until your bus departure time before you can get to Ollantaytambo. Factor this into your schedule, including possible delays, else you may miss your train to Machu Picchu. Train tickets to Machu Picchu can sell out weeks in advance, and missing your train can mess seriously with your travel plans.

Anton Swanepoel

The road to Ollantaytambo very well maintained and safe.

On the road, you will find some small stands where you can buy local items. Note, these are also available in Machu Picchu Pueblo.

Ollantaytambo

This town really got onto the map when the train service from
Cusco to Machu Picchu got disrupted, and most train services
stopped from Cusco. The majority of trains now depart from
Ollantaytambo. The town has its own ruins that surprisingly are
more expensive to visit than Machu Picchu. There is currently no
limit on the number of people visiting the ruins, and one can
purchase tickets at the site itself.

If coming by taxi you will be dropped off at the main plaza. By bus,
you will be dropped off right by the ruins that are across from the
plaza, over a steel bridge, by the craft market. Shops line the edges
of the plaza. Ollantaytambo is 75 kilometers (46 miles) from Cusco
by road. Interestingly, the same distance that Machu Picchu is from
Cusco, if taken as a direct flight.

Ollantaytambo Plaza.

Ruins, and craft market.

The ruins are spectacular themselves, and worth it if you have the time to visit them. Entry tickets are at the gate, which is located to the far back and right in the previous photo.

To get to the train station and train ticket offices for both Inca and Peru Rail, turn left just after crossing the steel bridge, before going to the ruins. Note, that you have to bring your train booking receipt and passport with you, including the credit or debit card that the ticket was purchased with. You will then be issued your train tickets. It does not matter if the card you bought your ticket with is expired by the time you pick your tickets up. They are a bit fussy, and for fraud do not normally accept a purchase if the person whose credit or debit card was used is not present at the time of collecting the tickets. The road to the train station is lined with restaurants and hotels, with the train platform right at the bottom of the road. The restaurants in town have free Wi-Fi, and serve good food.

Train departures are is at the bottom of the road. Both Inca and Peru Rail depart from here.

Pictured before, the train platform for departures and arrivals to and from Machu Picchu Pueblo is at the bottom of the road. Both Inca (www.incarail.com) and Peru Rail (www.perurail.com) depart from here. Taxi operators wait by the gates. On your return from Machu Picchu you can easily get a reasonably priced taxi directly to Cusco airport.

Train to Machu Picchu Pueblo (Aguas Calientes)

Once you go through security at the bottom of the road, you will be next to the train tracks, so watch your step. You are not normally allowed to enter unless your train is due within the next 20 minutes or so. The trains have letters or numbers on them, and you will be directed to your car depending on the ticket you purchased. For Inca Rail, the seats are numbered, and you are assigned a fixed seat. It is worth it to purchase the executive seat for the small up charge. The seats are the same size for normal and executive; however, in executive there are fewer seats and more leg space, and the seats are arranged four together around a table.

There is a small waiting area with a cafeteria next to the train tracks.

Pictured above, Executive car on Inca Rail. Note that the train tracks are very uneven and the cars do shake to and fro. If you are prone to motion sickness, you may want to take some precaution before the trip. See my book, 'Sea and Motion Sickness' *http://antonswanepoelbooks.com/motion_sickness.php* for precautionary measures and help with motion sickness. The train ride is around 1½ hours.

The train track runs along the river, and the view is spectacular. Make sure you have your camera ready. Depending on the time of the year, you will see the surrounding large mountain tops covered in snow.

Image from freeimages.

At times you may spot backpackers doing the Inca Trail.

Anton Swanepoel

Small shops along the train tracks cater to hikers doing the Inca Trail.

A little peek at what you will see on your way to Machu Picchu Pueblo.

Note that return train tickets sell out faster than the tickets to Machu Picchu. This is due to people hiking the Inca trail to Machu Picchu and then use the train to return. Thus, if you check and find a ticket towards Machu Picchu, do not assume that there will be one available for your return, confirm first.

Machu Picchu Pueblo (Aguas Calientes)

After 1½ hours of scenic train riding, you will arrive at Machu Picchu Pueblo, the closest town to Machu Picchu ruins. The town is expanding at a rapid rate, and in the last two years has seen some major growth. Although the town does not have the old and historical feel of Ollantaytambo, as it is mainly a tourist town, it still has a special character that is worthwhile exploring. When booking train tickets, some websites call it different names, and it can be confusing if you are going to the town or the ruins, however, all trains end up in the same place when you go to the ruins, being the town Machu Picchu Pueblo.

The trains do not always stop in the same place in the town. Sometimes they stop at the fountain, and other times they stop down the track near the end of the town - go figure. This, however, is not a problem as the town is easy to navigate, and if you are staying in a hotel or have booked a guided trip, a representative will normally wait for you and greet you as you depart from the train. Machu Picchu Pueblo is the closest you can stay to the ruins, unless you stay at the Sanctuary Lodge, which is right by the entry gates of the ruins. However, expect to pay US $500 or more a night to stay at the Lodge. Machu Picchu Pueblo is either a 30-minute bus ride or a one to two hour hike from the ruins. Located at the base of the mountain, it is next to the Urubamba River (Vilcanota). There are a number of hotels, bed & breakfasts and hostels in the town. Personally, if you can afford it, rather stay in a hotel than a hostel.

Both *www.bookings.com* and *www.expedia.com* offer the ability to book rooms in hotels and hostels. I personally used www.bookings.com and had excellent results. The price was quoted in US$ and on settling my bill the hotel ran my debit (visa) card in US$ without a problem. There are automatic teller machines in Machu Picchu Pueblo, and they accept Visa and Master card (debit or credit cards), and dispense local currency (Sol). Many shops will change US$ and some other currency for you to local Sol. However, most shops, hotels and restaurants accept Visa and Master card.

The train normally stops opposite the fountain. The path next to the fountain, going up, leads to the market, rest of the town, and to the train departure's area. Looking down at the fountain, to the right of the fountain is a bridge over the river and a road leading down towards the bus pickup and the ruins. To the left of the fountain are many of the hotels that are situated next to the train tracks. Looking back up and past the fountain, you will see a water channel that feeds the fountain when it rains. The channel that feeds the fountain ends in the form of two snakes, and encircles the fountain. Incas believed that the condor represents heaven, the puma earth, and the snake the underworld. Snakes are seen as messengers of the realm of the undead.

Trains normally stop here.

Pictured above, when turning left at the fountain where the trains normally stop, you will see the train tracks running through the bottom part of the town. Many of the hotels are along this road. As can be seen, the train tracks are right by the shops, so watch yourself when a train comes in.

Tickets for Machu Picchu

To enter the ruins at Machu Picchu, you need a ticket that is purchased in your name and linked to your passport number. Tickets are not available at the entry gate to Machu Picchu, and you cannot enter without a ticket in your name, and a valid passport or other government issued identification.

If you do not have a ticket already for Machu Picchu, then you can buy one at the local office in Machu Picchu Pueblo. Note that there is a limit of 2500 tickets per day to enter the ruins. In the busy seasons, tickets sell out months in advance. It is possible to get a ticket for the same day in the slow season, especially in September, but do not bargain on it.

The easier option is to buy your ticket online. One option is to buy it directly from the government website *www.machupicchu.gob.pe*

Alternatively, you can use any one of a number of tour companies listed under the Consultas Agencias / Authorized payment offices on the Ministry of Culture's website: www.machupicchu.gob.pe

I personally used *http://www.ticket-machupicchu.com/* and highly recommend them. After paying them for your ticket and a small handling fee, they will personally purchase your ticket and respond back to you in a few days with a PDF scan of your ticket. You can print this out and use it to enter the ruins without any worry.

If you are in Cusco, and have a few days, you can purchase tickets directly from the Ministry of Culture in Cusco.
Av. La Cultura #238 Condominio Huascar-Wanchaq
Monday through Friday from 8:00 a.m. until 6:30 p.m.
Saturday from 9:00 a.m. to noon.
Closed on holidays.

Alternatively, you can have a travel agency or your hotel in Cusco purchase the tickets for you.

Note, the access to both Mountain Machu Picchu and Mountain Huayna Picchu is restricted; you need to ask to have that added to your ticket at the time of purchase. You can no longer get the addition at the entry gate. If that addition (at an extra fee) is not added to your ticket at the time of purchase, you will not be allowed to climb the mountains.

The ticket office in Machu Picchu Pueblo is through the plaza, next to a church, see the following picture.

Note that the ticket office only accept local Sol currency.

The ticket office is next to the church on the right.

Machu Picchu Pueblo to Machu Picchu Ruins

The last leg of your adventure is to get to the ruins 450 meters (1476 feet) above you on a mountain ridge. This can be done by either taking a bus or hiking up.

The hiking trail follows mostly the same switchback road that the busses use to reach the ruins, with places where you cross over the road and climb a few steps up to the next level, only to cross the road repeatedly. The climb will take one to two hours to do, depending on your fitness level. Expect to arrive sweating and covered in dust at the entry point to the ruins. The view from the trail is in some parts very good; however, you can see the same view from the ruins. As mentioned before, forget about trying to hike up the mountain to see the sun come up at the ruins, as most of the time it is covered in mist and direct sunlight only hits Machu Picchu later in the morning.

Do realize that Machu Picchu was built on a mountain, and seeing the ruins requires you to climb up and down steps, and may not be fun if you are knackered after hiking up. I suggest to rather take an early bus up and first hike one of the two mountains, and then go and see the ruins. Mountain Machu Picchu is higher and takes longer in addition to being more difficult to climb, but is more rewarding. If you are not fit, I suggest Mountain Huayna Picchu, which is a 45-minute climb.

At the time of writing, bus tickets were US $17 return and US $9 one way. The gates open at 6am, with the first bus arriving at the gate just before 6am. In most cases, regardless if you arrived by bus or hiked, you will be outside the ruins while the sun is already up.

It takes around 30 minutes from the main entrance gate to the gates to climb either mountain. However, the gates to climb the mountains only open at 7am, so slow down a bit and enjoy the view on your way to climb the mountain.

Bus tickets from Machu Picchu Pueblo to Machu Picchu Ruins are sold at an office a little up the road away from the fountain where the trains stop. The ticket is valid for three days so it pays to purchase tickets in advance if you are staying multiple days. If this ticket office is closed, there is a second one just a little further up the road, by the bridge on the opposite side of the street. Pictured next, the ticket office for bus tickets to the ruins. The bus stop is directly down (across the train tracts) in the same road as the ticket office.

Ticket office for buses up to the ruins.

The bus station is only a short walk from the train stop. The busses pull up next to a small sign and will depart when full. If you want to be the first on the bus in the morning, then you need to be at the pickup point roughly one hour or so before the first bus leaves at 5:30am. The nearby shops open from around 5am and you can get some snacks and water, including coffee and sandwiches. The owners walk around between the lines selling their services, so no need to leave your spot to get breakfast.

Pictured above, Peru three-point turn reduced to two-point turn by reversing until the bus comes to an abrupt stop. Hope the road edge is strongly built.

The busses turn around just after the ticket office (yellow building on the right bottom of the photo). The road down leads to the bus station, camp grounds, museum and ruins. The market is to the left, across the river, and a bit down. The hot springs is behind the view of the camera, up the road.

Really fancy bus stop. ☺

If you do not immediately need to go and catch a bus, or have returned from the ruins, then you can explore the town a bit.

For those that are planning to use the campgrounds, head past the bus stop, down the road (about 20 to 30 minutes slow hike) to the bottom of the road just by the large bridge that crosses the river, near the museum. There is a large grass area where you can put up your tent. Being next to the river, I suggest you get plenty of mosquito repellent. Note, you have to pay a small fee to use the campgrounds, around 15 to 20 Sol a night per tent.

Chapter 5: Machu Picchu Pueblo (Aguas Calientes)

Machu Picchu Pueblo, is the gateway town of Machu Picchu Ruins. The town is an ever expanding town, and mostly centered on catering for tourists visiting the ruins. The town has stunning views of the surrounding mountains, and is split in two by a river with a number of bridges running across the river.

The local craft market in Machu Picchu Pueblo is very impressive for such a small town, possibly due to the large amount of tourists the town receives. You can get anything from necklaces, arm bands, earrings, to lama hair socks and jerseys to books and other souvenirs. Almost all shops and hotels have free Wi-Fi, and there are a number of Internet Cafes that can even download pictures from your digital camera and burn them onto a CD for you. There is a police station in the Plaza, and a number of good chemists (drug stores). ATMs dispense local SOL, but most shops, hotels and restaurants accept US$, and Visa or Master Card. Many shops will exchange US$ to local SOL.

There are many pizza places, with other places serving Chinese and Italian food. In general, the food is reasonably good, but seems to be European portions, small. If you are staying a day or two, I highly recommend an Indian hot rock massage.

Recycling is big in Peru and even in Machu Picchu. Please use the trash bins in the town and note that trash is separated between organic and non-organic. There are no trash bins in the ruins themselves. They generally do not allow you to take in just a plastic bag, so take a backpack and then put all your trash in a plastic bag inside your backpack. The town has a good sports field, if you feel like taking on the locals.

The sports field splits the top part of the town in two, with housing for locals working in the town behind the field against the mountain, and the tourist area with hotels and restaurants in front of the field.

Water channel ending in the form of a snake's head.

From the fountain where the train stops, head directly up to get to the local crafts market, or the departure's area for trains leaving the town.

When walking between the stalls in the craft market beware of the steps, as the craft market is built on a slope, due to the whole town being built on a hill. Actually, walking around the town is an endless up and down process.

A large rug found in the local craft market.

For the spiritual seeker, there is a large assortment of crystals, necklaces, armbands and more.

Anton Swanepoel

At the top of the market, to the far right when going up, you will see a small passage as pictured here, leading down. The train tracts will be on the left of the passage. Follow this passage down to the departure's area for all trains leaving the town. There is a small cafeteria inside, where you can purchase snacks and drinks while you wait for your train. A lovely garden is directly outside the departure's area. (Pictured next.)

To reach the plaza, walk left away from the fountain (when looking up towards the town from where the trains stop) over the bottom bridge, while following the train tracks. The first road up will be 'Antisuyo', take this or the second road up, 'Collasuyo', and you will get to the plaza. See the map section later in the book. There is a large statue of Pachacutec in the center of the plaza.

Pictured next, the Police station in the back right corner of the plaza. To the left of the police station is a drugstore and some restaurants. The church is next to the police station with the ticket office for Machu Picchu tickets next to the church. Remember to bring your passport.

Restaurants in the plaza.

Statue of Pachucuti.

The Incas called themselves the children of the sun. Pachucuti / Pachacutec (transformer of the earth) is seen as the founder of the once powerful Inca Empire, after he defeated the San in 1438ad. Interestingly, even with the rapid expansion, the Inca Empire was known for its peace and prosperity. Many of the buildings in Cusco rest on foundations built over 500 years ago by Pachucuti.

Anton Swanepoel

For over 3000 years some of the most advanced civilizations ruled the mountains and coasts of Peru. The Inca Empire was the last and greatest of the great civilizations to rule this land. They conquered the entire Andean region.

Pachucuti (ruled 1438–1471/1472) was the leader who had the vision to expand the Inca Empire from Cusco. Although Pachucuti was the son of the emperor, he was not the heir to the throne. The Incas were attacked by the Chankas in 1438, under the leadership of Hanan Chanka "Anccu Hualloc," who commanded almost 40 000 warriors. The Chankas were a fierce force and bloody in battle. Captured enemies were often scalped or skinned alive. They often made cups from their enemies' skulls, and drank their blood from it. The Chankas believed that their ancestors were still with them, and carried their mummified bodies into battle to assist them. The mummified corpse of the leader who began the expansion of the Chankas, Uscovilca, was carried into the battle against the Incas.

During the battle for Cusco, all was nearly lost for the Incas, and the emperor, Inca Viracocha and most of the nobility fled the battle. The young prince, Pachacuti Inca Yupanqui or Pachacutec, took a small detachment of warriors and focused their efforts on capturing Uscovilca's mummified corpse. They succeeded in toppling the mummy from its litter. The Chankas were so shocked that their revered ancestor was captured, that they immediately surrendered to the Incas.

Pachucuti took the throne, and portrayed himself as the living embodiment of the Sun God. He changed the religion from mainly worshiping ancestors, to worshiping the sun and the moon. It is believed that Pachucuti had Machu Picchu constructed as a royal estate. When Pachucuti died, his corpse was mummified. It is believed the corpse was left out in the sun by day, then frozen overnight. With the repeated heating, freezing and thawing, the corpse would become desiccated. This is also how Peruvians preserve lama meat. Interestingly, the result is jerky, one of a few Quechua words used in English.

Although there are shops and restaurants on the upper part of the town, many of the shops selling souvenirs are below by the train tracts. Watch yourself when you are in the lower parts of the town near the train tracks, I promise you the train is tougher than you.

Many of the restaurants are situated near the plaza, with a few further down along the road next to the train tracks. For an upmarket restaurant, follow the road running next to the train tracts on the opposite side of the craft market, until you come to this bridge. The restaurant is across the bridge on the right. The restaurant has links to Inkaterra, Machu Picchu Pueblo Hotel, which is opposite of the restaurant.

There are police and security all over the town, and in general, the town is very safe, even late at night. Still, do not carelessly leave your valuables openly on a table in a restaurant or in your room when you are out.

Chapter 6: Machu Picchu Ruins

Machu Picchu is 75 kilometers (46 miles) as the crow flies, from Cusco. Being around 914 meters (3000 feet) lower, Machu Picchu is warmer than Cusco in the winter.

Mystical Machu Picchu is 2430 meters (7972 feet) up in the mountains, 450 meters (1476 feet) above the sacred Urubamba River. There are over 200 structures at the site, most made from white granite. Some of the stones are almost 4 meters (13 feet) high, and weigh more than 20 tones. The builders of Machu Picchu, accomplished this magnificent feat without any steel tools, wheels or pulleys. It is believed that the workers used river rocks, to shape the stones by chipping piece by piece away.

The current believe is that Machu Picchu was constructed around 1450, by Pachucuti, as a royal estate. This comes from a number of evidence found at Machu Picchu such as the building style that corresponds to other buildings known to have been constructed by Pachucuti, and a Spanish register, held in the colonial archives in Cusco, dated 1568, that actually mentions the town called Picchu, and a clear reference to its owner, Inca Yupanqui, also known as Pachucuti. The document was found in the late 1980s, by Berkeley anthologist John H. Rowe. The document is from a legal dispute where the Pachucuti family asked for a return of lands that belonged to the lineage of the Pachucuti family. With the direct mention of the town called Picchu and a royal estate, as well as referencing the location mentioned in the document to known sites, the document seems to strongly refer to Machu Picchu.

It should be noted that from archaeological evidence, Machu Picchu, as well as Pisac and Ollantaytambo, were used as ceremonial sites, centuries (some say millennia) before the Inca, and actually had existing structures that may have been used for ceremonial and astronomical purposes.

For interest, an ancient underwater temple around 1000 to 1500 old, was discovered in Lake Titicaca in 2000. The temple predates the Inca civilization and was perhaps built by the Tiwanaku people. The ruins are 200 meters by 50 meters large (656.2 feet by 164 feet). 200 dives have been made to the temple. A number of gold and stone artifacts were recovered from the temple. The team also found a terrace for crops, a long road, and an 800 meter (2624.7 feet) long wall under Lake Titicaca. Further research is underway.

Since Pachucuti was the living embodiment of the Sun God, any royal estate of his is of extreme importance, both spiritually as well as royally. This is evident in the level of detail and work that went into building Machu Picchu, that spans 13 km² (5 mi2). In February, 2010, David Crespy, a French engineer, was exploring Machu Picchu, when he saw a pile of rock that looked like a door, at the foot of one of the main buildings at the heart of Machu Picchu. Crespy alerted Thierry Jamin, a French researcher and explorer, and president of the Inkari Institute. During September and November of 2011, Thierry Jamin with other archaeologists, visited Machu Picchu and confirmed David Crespy's theory that it is indeed a doorway to a hidden chamber, very similar to burial sites that Thierry Jamin and his companions often discovered in the valleys of Lacco-Yavero and Chunchusmayo. The leading theory is that the site could possibly be a burial place.

On 22 March, 2012, the Peruvian Ministry of Culture granted Thierry Jamin and his team permission to do a series of electromagnetic surveys. The surveys reveal a staircase leading to an underground cavity. From 9 April to 17 April, 2012, the team did a number of surveys using a georadar (Golden King DPRP). The results confirmed the existence of two entrances, located behind the famous door, as well as a stairway leading to a main room, possibly a burial chamber. A few days later, the team reconfirmed their results by using a Rover CII New Edition and a CaveFinde device, used to specifically detect subterranean cavities. The new data shows that there are several cavities, with the main room being 3 x 3 meters (10 x 10 feet).

The data also shows the existence of metals such as gold and silver in great quantities. The metals are typical to a classic burial chamber, further suggesting the existence of graves filled with offerings. An endoscopic camera was then used to show that the stones at the 'door' do not support the building, but closes the entrance. For more information, see *http://www.machupicchu-ciudadela.com/en/*

This find sparked controversy, as the construction date of Machu Picchu is taken from the building style. A Wari tomb was discovered 281 kilometers (175 miles) north of Lima. The tomb housed 63 mummies, mostly woman, three of which are thought to be Wari queens. The tomb had more than 1,200 artifacts, including gold- and silver-inlaid jewelry, as well as ceremonial axes and looms. The Wari flourished from 500 AD to 1000 AD, well before the Inca. If the artifacts in the new chamber at Machu Picchu are similar to that of the Wari, it has the potential to rewrite the history of Machu Picchu.

For the spiritually interested, Machu Picchu lies right between two natural geological fault lines. The two mountains (mountain Machu Picchu and mountain Huayna Picchu) on either side of Machu Picchu is actually the sides that stood standing of the ridgeline when the part Machu Picchu is on, sank down. Machu Picchu is also said to lie directly on top of a major earth energy vortex, and close to earth's sacral chakra situated at Lake Titicaca.

The electromagnetic subterranean energy at Machu Picchu is said to be a powerful healing and spiritual awakening, energy. Machu Picchu is aligned with The Great Pyramid of Giza, as well as other ancient sites such as the Nazca lines and Easter Island, along a straight line around the center of the Earth, within a margin of error of less than one-tenth of one degree of latitude, called the great circle.

This circle has its axis point in southeastern Alaska, with all the sites at an equally distant from the axis point at one-quarter of the circumference of the earth. Machu Picchu lies on a north-south line that can be drawn between Mount Huayna Picchu and Mount Salcantay, one of the most revered apus in Inca cosmology. Atop the peak of Huayna Picchu, is an arrow-shaped stone that points due south, directly through the Intihuatana Stone, to Mount Salcantay. An east-west line runs from Machu Picchu, to Mount San Miguel, another revered apus in Inca cosmology. The Southern Cross shines directly above the holy mountain that overlooks the site. The easiest place to reach to see these alignments are atop Mount Machu Picchu.

These alignments and the position of Machu Picchu, brought about a new theory as to its purpose. Italian archaeoastronomer (the investigation of the astronomical knowledge of prehistoric cultures) Giulio Magli suggests that Machu Picchu may be the end of a ceremonial journey that echoed a celestial journey. The Inca Trail from Cusco, was to prepare the pilgrims for entry into Machu Picchu, with the final point being the Intihuatana Stone, the highest spot at Machu Picchu ruins.

It is estimated that it took at least 50 years to build Machu Picchu. However, it was abandoned shortly after it was built. The leading theory as to why, is because of lack of food and support. With Machu Picchu being a royal estate of Pachucuti, who died possibly of smallpox, the empire was at war with his two sons fighting for the crown. The Spanish invaded Peru soon afterwards, causing more fighting, not the circumstances in which royal estates are visited or maintained. It is generally thought that Machu Picchu was in use from 1450 to 1540, and had a standard population of 300 that rose to 750 when the emperor was in residence.

Machu Picchu gate / Cafeteria

Regardless of whether you hiked up or took a bus up, your first stop will be the gate and cafeteria. Pictured above, Machu Picchu gate is on the second level, steps are to the right leading down to the toilets and bus pick up and drop off area. There are no toilets in the ruins, so go before you enter; else you will have to come all the way back to use a toilet. In the back of the photo to the right is a small cafeteria and souvenir shop. Where the umbrellas are in the back is a small eating area for food you buy at the cafeteria.

The gates are open from 6am to 5pm, and there are about four lanes where your passport and ticket get scanned. If you used one of the Internet companies that purchased the tickets for you, then fear not. The printed out barcode ticket from them is almost exactly what you will get from the official office. Remember to take water (at least two liters per person for a morning if you plan to climb the mountain, and 1 liter if just milling around the ruins) and a light snack. You need your passport to enter the ruins. Do not leave it in the hotel.

Anton Swanepoel

There is a booth where you can leave your hiking bags if you want to. There is also a stand with a stamp where you can stamp your passport to brag that you were at Machu Picchu. Note, it is technically illegal for you to stamp your passport, so if you do stamp your passport, select a page that has a few stamps in order to make it less obvious to customs. After you pass the gate, you can hire a guide if you elect to do so, or go on your own steam. Remember to use the toilets before you go in! Cost is one Sol for entrance to the toilet, and remember to grab some toilet paper at the ticket booth before you go in, as there is no toilet paper inside.

Pictured next is the lower level of the entry gate to Machu Picchu ruins. Between midday and 3pm, the queue to get a bus can be long, and you can easily wait half an hour to get on, so factor this into your travel time, including the 30-minute bus ride back. After 4pm the queue is short, and by 5pm, you should have no problem hopping on a bus within minutes. Note, the last bus leaves at 5:30pm, if you miss that you are walking back. All the people standing in line from directly in front of the camera, all the way anticlockwise to the last person, are waiting for a bus.

Lower level of the entry gate to Machu Picchu ruins.

Names of Objects and Places in the Ruins

Note, any names given to stones and buildings are in most cases from what Hiram Bingham named them. The functions of these objects are also in most cases from what he concluded they were used for. The actual fact is that we have no concrete evidence as to what most of the objects were used for or their actual names. For many of the objects, you may hear a number of different stories for their use, depending on the creativeness of the guides. I have included the most accepted names and descriptions of objects, including actual archeological and scientific evidence found pertaining to each object or building.

Interestingly, in January 2010, around 2000 tourists and as many locals were trapped when the roads and railway were damaged during heavy rains. The people were airlifted out, and repairs were started. Machu Picchu remained closed until 1 April 2010.

Hiram Bingham was an American explorer and professor of history at Yale University. In 1911, Bingham came to Peru in search of the fabled lost city, Vilcabamba. Bingham followed a path the Peruvian government had recently cut into the cloud forest to assist with trade. After a few days trek, Bingham camped near the river at the base of Machu Picchu. A local, living in a hut nearby, told him that there were ruins on the mountain. On the morning of 25 July, 1911, he and his guide climbed for over two and a half hours to the top, where they found a family living there. After a short break, a young boy volunteered to take Bingham further, and show him the ruins.

Bingham took pictures of the site but then left it, as he was in search of Vilcabamba and did not originally think Machu Picchu to be of much importance. He continued exploring the region, not even bothering to take his companions to see Machu Picchu, as his heart was set on Vilcabamba. Bingham found a number of other ruins, but eventually gave up looking for the fabled last Inca city. The next year, Bingham returned with a crew to excavate Machu Picchu. In total, over 120 gold, silver, ceramic, bone and textile works were found, which included pottery, stone tools, and even bronze knives, as well as a number of burial sites. Bingham went on to become a senator and played a major role in the excavation of Machu Picchu, while longing to have discovered Vilcabamba.

Ironically, in the late 1960s, American adventurers Antonio Santander and Gene Savoy found the real Vilcabama at a place called Espiritu Pampa (plane of the ghosts), 80 kilometers (50 miles) northwest of Machu Picchu, by following Bingham's original exploration. Bingham did discover the site, but it was so overgrown that he could see little of it, and thought it to be of little value. Professor Edmundo Guillen found letters in a Museum in Seville (a city of southwest Spain) that describes the city of Vilcabamba. In 1976, Guillen went to the city and compared the letter with the site, finding that Espiritu Pampa is Vilcabamba. Archeologist Vincent Lee and John Hemming excavated areas in Vilcabamba, confirming its identity.

After passing through the ticket check point, you will ascend a number of steps, and then arrive at a walkway that affords you a stunning view of the river below.

As soon as you round the corner, Machu Picchu jumps out at you, taking your breath away.

Anton Swanepoel

Distant view of the ruins.

There are three paths you can take, long (about three hours), medium (about two hours) or short (about one hour), all marked. The long path starts to the left just as you see the first ruins. This is the path I suggest you use, and the one you need to take if you want to climb either mountain, see the Inti Punku, the Inca Bridge, the Funeral Rock, and the Intiwatana (the Hitching Post of the Sun). The two thatched buildings pictured before, are thought to have possibly been granaries.

This is the view that you will see when looking up just as you near the first ruins. The path that the people are taking in the back to the left is the longer route and the one to follow. Do make a stop at the hut to inspect the roof. This building at current is one of a few that had its roof restored. It is thought that the building could have been used as a granary. This high up in the mountains, there is a huge problem with strong winds. The thatched roofs had to be latched to the building by using stone pegs sticking out at the sides of the buildings.

Anton Swanepoel

At the granary, continued up to the Funeral Rock. Mountain Machu Picchu and the Sun Gate are behind this view. You will see a path that looks like the one you are standing on now, just a little way up, leading away to the mountain.

Pictured next, a little way up on the path, this is the view that will greet you. The pyramid-like structure in the middle left is where Intiwatana is. To climb Mountain Huayna Picchu, you have to go past that, and all the way to the back and right of the photo.

Machu Picchu is divided into two key districts by the large grassy square. On the left of the square are the Royal and Sacred areas where it is believed the Inca ruler, and his court resided. To the right is the area where it is believed the workers lived, also called the Urban or Industrial Sector. Pottery, stone tools, and even bronze knives, were found in this area. Tip, turn your head sideways, and you will see Mountain Huayna Picchu in the back making a face.

Cover Image from Fotolia.

Interestingly, Machu Picchu is supplied with water by a man-made fountain nearby. One of the fronts of the two fault lines, is a giant slope of granite from Mountain Machu Picchu, which often has its top covered in mist and clouds. The water that runs down the mountain, is collected behind a 14.5 meter (47 feet) long wall. The water slowly seeps through the wall and collects in a basin at the bottom, then runs along a 750 meter (2475 feet) canal to Machu Picchu. The canal runs at a 3% grade to the city, and can deliver 23 to 114 liters of water a minute, depending on the season. The canal ends at the emperor's house in a fountain, from where it continues through the city to in total, 16 fountains. The water spouts in the fountains were designed in such a way that the water spilled away from the wall, allowing easy filling of water jugs. The water is enough to sustain up to 1000 people.

Anton Swanepoel

Machu Picchu viewed sideways with Huayna Picchu smiling at you.

Just before you get to the Guard House and Funeral Rock, you will pass a large grass area. This is open for resting and picnic if you want. Continue going up to the right to see the Guard House, Funeral Rock, Barracks, Upper Cemetery and path to the Inca Bridge or to continue to the rest of the ruins and to climb Mountain Huayna Picchu.

Funeral Rock

The Funeral Rock got its name from Harem Bingham, who discovered a number of skeletons in 1912, in the area behind the Funeral Rock, indicating that the site may have been used as a funeral site. Sacrificing humans, especially children, to the mountain gods, was practiced by the Inca. A number of mummified human remains have been found at several locations atop various mountains in Peru. Bingham thought that the Funeral Rock could have been used as a mortuary slab where the deceased were laid out to be mummified.

Funeral Rock.

The exact process of mummification is not known, but speculations are that it follows the same process of how the Peruvians today preserve lama meat, called jerky. The body is left out in the sun to dry out, then frozen during the night in the cold, in the day it thaws again in the sun. The repeated process of heating, freezing and thawing, mummifies the body.

It should be noted that no concrete evidence has been found indicating that the rock was used in any funeral or sacrifice role. However, what is interesting to note is the three steps at the right-hand side, which corresponds to the steps carved into the rock in the Royal Tomb (Pachamama's Cave). These three steps are believed to represent the underworld, earth, and heaven. (The top part is not seen as a step but the top of the rock).

In total, 177 remains were found all over Machu Picchu, in over 100 burial sites. Bingham's bone expert on the expedition, Dr. George Eaton, examined the remains and wrongly concluded that over 80% of the bodies were of women. His mistake was due to his limited compare sample he had.

Eaton's conclusion led Bingham to reason that the remains were that of the so called, Virgins of the Sun, chosen to be offered to the Sun God. The Incas did take the most beautiful girls of royalty and offered them to the Gods. However, Bingham's theory was wrong. The bones were re-examined by forensic anthropologist John Verano with modern equipment. He found that the sexes of the skeletons were almost 50/50, and included a number of children. To determine the sex of a skeleton, you have to compare it to many ethnic and racial groups. However, Eaton only had access to European and African descent data, and not the smaller Peruvian descent. The people in the Andes are more delicately built as well as shorter, leading Eaton to miscalculate the sex of many of the remains.

John Verano found no evidence of violent injury on the skeletons at Machu Picchu, suggesting they were not offered. In addition, the burials were simple with no high-value artifacts, suggesting they were not royalty or religious leaders. From their bones and joints, Verano found that they were not common laborers doing hard work, but from a middle class. Almost no arthritis were found even in the older adults among the skeletons. Through a technique called isotopic analysis, their diet was established. A small sample of bone is vaporized, and the chemical traces of food that were absorbed into the bones are then analyzed. Among the vaporized particles, a high percentage of carbon-13 isotopes were found. Carbon-13 isotopes is the signature of corn. In Inca times, corn was a royal food and not as common as today. Corn is rich in carbohydrates, which is bad for your teeth. Many of the remains showed signs of numerous cavities, abscesses and lost teeth. So, although they were not royalty, they ate royal food.

These findings, together with other evidence, strongly suggest that Machu Picchu was a royal retreat for the emperor and that the remains are that of caretakers of Machu Picchu and servants of the emperor.

Semicircular Terraces / Guard House

View of the Guard House (Caretaker's Hut, also called, House of the Guardians). The Funeral Rock is just to the right of the photo, with the ruins down to the left. The path to the Inca Bridge is behind you. The 10 windows and Barracks are on the terrace just to the right of the photo. This view shows the semicircular terraces to the left. Hikers who did the Inca trail, will arrive at the hut, coming from the Inti Punku (The Door of the Sun).

It should be noted that at this point, you are not inside Machu Picchu itself, but outside the city walls, and still need to pass through the doorway.

Hiram Bingham gave the name to this hut as he thought the hut could have been used by Inca warriors to guard the entrance to Machu Picchu. This theory is supported by the nearby structure that is thought to have been a barracks. Note the steps leading down from the hut to the terraces. You can rest or meditate on the terraces.

Interestingly, the terraces are not unique to Machu Picchu. Several other ruins have terraces as well. The terraces at Pisac, called Inca Písac, span up the mountain to a height of 3000 meters (9842 feet). At Machu Picchu, there are over 600 terraces. The terraces are on average around 2.1 meters (7 feet) high, and 3 meters (10 feet) wide. The terraces are sloped backwards at a 5 degree angle. This allows the weight of the sand and gravel of the terraces to be forced downwards, anchoring Machu Picchu. Without the terraces, Machu Picchu would have slid off the mountain long ago. The terraces as well as the buildings in Machu Picchu are linked together with over 3000 steps.

The terraces are made of course rocks at the bottom, followed by finer rocks and gravel, then sand, and lastly topsoil. Apart from anchoring Machu Picchu, the terraces served two additional purposes. Firstly, they slowed and controlled the 200 mm (76 inches) of rainfall a year that occurs at Machu Picchu, stopping erosion from occurring as well as any mudslides. Water slowly seeps through the topsoil down to the rocks below, and then through one of the 130 drains placed around Machu Picchu. The water is then channeled to the Dirt Ditch, where the water flows down to the river below. The result is that you never see pools of water standing at Machu Picchu, no matter how hard it rains.

The second use for the terraces was farming. The topsoil for the terraces were brought basket by basket from the flood plains below near the river. In the mid-1990s, soil samples from the terraces were analyzed and proved that maze was the primary crop grown at Machu Picchu, along with potatoes and avocados. In total, Machu Picchu had 12 acres of terraced lands on which to grow crops.

It is calculated that the terraces could only support 55 people with food. It is thought that additional food was brought from the nearby town of Patallaqta (Llaqtapata), a few hours walk from Machu Picchu.

During the day, the terraces absorbed heat from the sun. At night, the terraces radiated the heat back into the earth, warming Machu Picchu and protecting the crops.

Barracks and Upper Cemetery

View of the Barracks (also called 10 windows) and Upper Cemetery from next to the Funeral Rock. To go to the Inca Bridge, continue, passing by the right of the Upper Cemetery. Hiram Bingham christened the large flat area the Upper Cemetery, due to the large amount of skeletons he uncovered on his return trip in 1912.

You can climb onto the terraces by the Barracks to have a magnificent view of Machu Picchu with Mountain Huayna Picchu in the back. This area is one of the more silent places to mediate at. Pictured next, the view from the top of the Barracks.

Inca Doorway

From the Guard House, a path leads down to the Inca Doorway. The doorway is one of the main entrances to the ruins and could be barricaded closed from the inside. Although no evidence has been found of fighting at Machu Picchu, it seems that some though to its defense was given with the doorway, and Inca Bridge that could be dismantled. Although none of the bodies at Machu Picchu showed signs of trauma, a grave with nine bodies was found at Patallaqta (town that supplied Machu Picchu with food) by archaeologist Fernando Astete (director of the Machu Picchu archeological park), and fellow archaeologist Elva Torres. All the remains showed signs of trauma, mainly from blunt objects such as clubs. A large number also had skull surgery, called trepanation where a hole is cut into the skull to release intracranial pressure due to skull fractures. The Incas practiced this procedure with a very high degree of success. It is though that these nine were soldiers and may have been in a skirmish in defending the nearby area, possibly even Machu Picchu.

Inca Doorway.

Rooms on both sides of the passage.

Picture of one of the rooms. Keep going past the rooms, down to the quarry.

Quarry

Pictured above, the rock quarry. This was the main site were the rocks making up Machu Picchu were sourced, as well as cut to fit where needed. Some of the rocks are in partial preparation to be cut into stone blocks. Some of the stones at Machu Picchu weighed up to 20 tons, and were lifted up to 3 meters (10 feet) onto other stones.

The stones were hand carved to fit adjacent stones, so precise that a knife blade cannot pass between them. The larger stones were placed on top of each other, with no mortar. Some buildings of a different style, with smaller rocks, did use mortar made from clay, earth, and small stones. It is believed that workers used hard river rocks, to gradually chip away at the granite stones until they got a rough shape they wanted. The stone was then chiseled down with progressively smaller river rocks, taking off less and less at a time to enhance precision. The angle of the strike was also important. If stuck at a steep angle while flicking the wrist at the moment of impact, large flakes of granite can be chipped away. If striking the rock head on, only small flakes sometimes the size of dust, were flaked off.

Here you can see a stone slab left in partial preparation. The stone was carefully split into smaller workable pieces.

When viewing the stones, one will find that although they perfectly fit the stone next to them, they are not square. It is believed that the workers may have used a method called scribing.

This method is sometimes used by log cabin builders to fit irregular log cabin surfaces. Workers would transfer the face of one stone to the side of another stone, using a protractor and small river rocks as hammers. This allowed the two stones to perfectly match against each other. Big stones were rested on each other, and then the top stone was tilted up and propped in place with wooden poles, to allow workers to chisel the bottom part, until it fitted perfectly. The stone would have needed to be tilted up and dropped down a number of times to check the fit.

The question arose as to how the builders managed to move the large stones from the quarry to their places. One theory is that they used ropes weaved from plant and animal fibers and dragged the stones around, possibly shaping the bottom to resemble a boat to allow for easier transportation, as well as using logs, pebbles and mud to roll the large stones on. This method is known to have been used at other ancient sites around the world. However, this theory causes a problem, as for it to work you require a sizable work force and a large area to work in. It is impossible to move large stones in cramped places like Machu Picchu with this method.

In 1998, architect and ancient technology enthusiast, Vincle Lee, set out to prove a new theory. Lee and several volunteers conducted an experiment with a 13 ton block of marble. They placed the stone on a wooden sledge and moved it over a wooden ladder. The sledge and ladder had wooden poles sticking out the side, allowing Lee and the volunteers to drive poles between them, and wedge the stone forward. They managed to move the block of marble up a ramp with a 25% gradient, and then turned the stone 90 degrees in position, with such ease that it even astounded Lee. It is believed that the Incas used a similar process.

To spread the load of the massive stones throughout the building they were used for, the Incas alternated between placing stones vertically and horizontally.

If you think the stonework at Machu Picchu is impressive, you are going to have a field day at the mysterious and enigmatic ruins of Tiwanaku (Tiahuanaco), situated at 3962 meters (13 000 feet) above sea level, on the border of Bolivia and Peru. The ruins are close to Lake Titicaca, which is thought to have once extended up to the city. Tiwanaku was once a seaport, supporting a population of approximately 40,000 to 100,000 people. Docks lie in ruin, one so big that at its time could have accommodated hundreds of sea-going vessels. Part of what makes the ruins so enigmatic is that the stone blocks (Andesite granite) are so large, that even with modern technology, it would be a marvel to transport the blocks from their source, 80 kilometers (50 miles) away. Even though many of the blocks weigh upwards of 200 tons, they lie scatter like weeds in the wind (one block still in place weighs an estimated 440 tons). The largest helicopter in production today is the Mil Mi-26, capable of lifting 20 tons, with the experimental Mil Mi-12 capable of lifting 44 tons. The ruins are said to date to around 15,000 years ago, making them the oldest ruins in the world.

Of interest, some of the ruins are 6 meters (20 feet) underground. The leading explanation is that a massive flood (tidal wave) washed over the city, toppling the stone structures, as well as burying many under sand. The lost city of Atlantis possibly? ☺ This flooding could have happened with the Andean upheaval, which possibly caused a basin to form, flooding the now underwater ruins in Lake Titicaca, mentioned earlier. Noah's great flood? The stone blocks at Tiwanaku appear to have been machined, so perfect that even with modern equipment it would be difficult if not impossible to replicate. In fact, creating similar ruins would be impossible even today. One of the stones are covered in astrological information, so detailed in planetary bodily movements that it even baffles scholars today. Even 15,000 years ago, the inhabitants knew earth was round and the paths of distant planets. From the markings they knew the ratio of Pi and trigonometry. What is also astounding is that the Tiwanaku seems to not have any roots in the area nor any other place of known origin.

Pass through the quarry, towards the Principle Temple.

Just before turning left into the sacred plaza, you will have a good view of the Sacred Square.

Sacred Plaza / Main Temple

The Sacred Plaza consists of the Temple of Three Windows, the Principal Temple and the Intihuatana, and was named by Bingham. Due to their size he thought the area was the perfect place for ceremonies. The smaller room adjacent to the Main Temple was named the Sacristy by Bingham. He thought it to be the place where priests would prepare for a ceremony.

The temple is missing its fourth wall. Some say the reason is that Machu Picchu was never finished. More evidence that the builders were short on time, can be seen on the back of the main wall as shown in the previous picture. The right side of the wall is collapsing. Unlike other walls, this wall has no solid foundation, but only sand, that is giving in. It is theorized that time was a problem and sacrifices were made, with the result that the wall is collapsing. More evidence for uncompleted work can be seen from the large stone in the plaza that was still being worked on. Where this stone was supposed to be used, is a mystery.

Temple of the Three Windows

The temple of the three windows is to the right of the large stone, and overlooks the Sacred Square and Industrial Sector.

The Temple of the Three Windows actually has five windows; the side two are just closed off. As the other objects, the temple got its name from Bingham. The lintels in the temple are thought to weigh around three tons, a characteristic of imperial Inca architecture. Bingham believed that the three windows represented the three mythological caves at Tambotoco Hill. According to legend, the four Ayar brothers and their sisters stepped into the world from one of the caves. After a feud, where they locked one of their brothers up by tricking him to go back into the cave and then sealing the cave, they journeyed in search of a permanent settlement. Two brothers turned into stone and formed mountains on the way, leaving the last brother, Ayar Auca, to settle at Cusco and create the Inca Empire. Interestingly the Temple of the Three Windows holds inscriptions from Enrique Palma, Gabino Sánchez and Agustín Lizárraga, dating back to July 1901.

Enrique Palma, Gabino Sánchez and Agustín Lizárraga actually stayed at Machu Picchu in 1901 and recorded in their chronicles that local farmers were living at Machu Picchu at the time. A local farmer, Anacleto Alvarez, claimed to have been working the land in the vicinity of Machu Picchu for more than eight years. As mentioned earlier, even Bingham found a local family living at Machu Picchu, and it was one of the local boys who took Bingham to the ruins. However, it is still Hiram Bingham that brought Machu Picchu to the world's attention.

Broken pottery was found at and below the Temple of The Three Windows. The pottery is believed to have been broken during ritual ceremonies, giving further weight to the theory that the room was a Sacred Temple.

Chamber of Ornaments

While facing the main wall with the Temple of the three Windows to your right, pass by the left of the Principle Temple towards the Chamber of Ornaments. This interesting room was built in such a way that it echoes sound. The exact use for the room is unknown, but it is theorized that it could have been a prayer room where priests may have chanted incantations. The niches in the walls may have been used to hold sacred objects. Today, the room it is a favorite room for tourists to sing and hear an echo of their voices.

From the Chamber of Ornaments, continued going up to the Intiwatana.

Looking back at Machu Picchu just before reaching the Intiwatana. The Principle Temple is in the foreground of the picture.

Intiwatana / Intihuatana (Hitching Post of the Sun)

The famous Intiwatana, 2350 meters (7710 feet) above sea level.

The Intiwatana, is located at the highest point of the Machu Picchu Ruins, at the top of a large terraced pyramid, and was carved on site from one solid piece of granite. The tab on the opposite side of the flat step (altar) points towards magnetic north. It is believed that the stone may have been used for astronomical and religious purposes. The Quechua word Intihuatana translates to "hitching post of the sun," however, its actual purpose is unknown. The top of the rock is carved into a square, with the corners aligning to the four cardinal points. The north to east line of the flat side of the square marks the winter solstice (June 21), while the east to south marks the summer solstice (December 22). On winter solstice during sunrise the light projects though the Intihuatana to produce a triangle of light, which illuminates two strange concentric circles on the floor. This causes even more speculations as to the use of the rock, with some saying that it focusses the energy from the earth vortex, upon which Machu Picchu rests. The shape of the Intihuatana mimics the horn-shaped peak Huayna Picchu.

Archaeologists believe that the Intihuatana may have been used for astronomical observations and calculating the passing of time to allow them to predict when to plant crops. Spiritualists believe that the Incas tied up the setting solstice sun that they feared would disappear forever, and made sure it did not go too far away. The hitching of the sun was done on a physical and spiritual level, and forced the sun to go in a pattern they wanted. This way, the Incas believed they could control their destiny. It is also believed that the builders of Machu Picchu saw it as an axis mundi, a meeting of the heaven and the earth, where they can communicate with the Gods. Machu Picchu is seen as a spiritual union of the sky, river, and mountains. As mentioned before, sacred mountains lie at the compass points of Machu Picchu, while the Southern Cross shines directly above the holy mountain that overlooks the site. It is believed by some that in addition to worshiping the sun, rivers, and mountains as gods, the Inca derived power by being physically close to them, and that the Intihuatana was used to draw power from the sun in a ritual, giving them the power to expand the Empire at such an unprecedented rate.

Originally, people were allowed to touch and even conduct spiritual ceremonies on the rock, but nowadays the rock is roped off and no touching is allowed. A permanent security guard makes sure visitors adhere to the rules. On 8 September, 2000 a film crew was busy making a beer commercial at Machu Picchu. One of the arms of a crane fell onto the Intihuatana breaking a piece off. A worker was blamed for allowing the crew to film without the proper permission. However, I fail to see how the proper paperwork would have prevented the falling of the crane arm.

Interestingly, the Intihuatana at Machu Picchu was not the only one constructed. Almost every other major site in Peru had one, but were destroyed when the Spanish invaded Peru. Priests destroyed them due to believing that they possessed evil magic. The one at Machu Picchu is just the last known surviving one. It should be noted that Intihuatana is a modern name, no one knows what it was called originally. At midday on March 21st and September 21st, the sun stands almost directly above the Intihuatana, creating no shadow. From the Intihuatana, go down the interesting path to the Sacred Square / Principle Plaza.

Follow the path down, while enjoying the awesome view.

Sacred Square (Principal Plaza)

The Sacred Square is a smaller version of the one found at
Sacsayhuamán in Cusco, which holds the yearly Inti Raymi festival
during the month of June. It is possible that this square at Machu
Picchu was used for festivals, sports, or just to relax. However, the
square plays a very important role at Machu Picchu, by helping to
keep Machu Picchu securely on the mountain.

Sacred Square.

View from the Sacred Square towards the Intihuatana.

As mentioned before, Machu Picchu gets around 200mm (76 inches) of rain a year. Much of the water is channeled down the terraces and then down the Dirt Ditch to the river below. Machu Picchu itself has 130 drains around the site, with most of them draining into the Sacred Square.

From archeological studies, it was found that around 60% of Machu Picchu is actually underground. The entire Sacred Square was constructed with a layer of topsoil, followed by a layer of dirt, then gravel, then lastly a thick layer of white granite chips. This allows the water to drain away without causing erosion. The granite chips are believed to have come from the leftovers of carving the blocks to make the buildings. This drainage system extends around 2.7 meters (9 feet) below the surface and encompasses several hectares.

The Inti Raymi ritual was banned by the Catholic Church until the 1940s. The ritual is held on the June solstice. The last time before 1940 when it was seen, was by a young Spanish priest, father Cristopher, more than 400 years ago – 1536. Many scholars think that this ritual was performed at Machu Picchu. Inti Raymi actually translates to June. The Inca believed that the Sun was holding the celebration. The Inca and nobility were his guests. This is one of the most important rituals of the Inca, even today.

Sunken Square

Behind the Sacred Square, are a number of terraces that end in a sunken square. The exact role of the square is not known, as of yet, but it was possibly used for smaller function or to crow crops. Head past the sunken square to the Surveillance Place.

Path to the Surveillance Place.

Surveillance Place and Ceremonial Rock (Sacred Rock)

The Surveillance Place is right in front of the Sacred Rock, exactly at the most northern part of Machu Picchu. It is thought that the area may have been used for ceremonial purposes, with the two adjoining buildings (huayranas) possibly housing sacred artifacts.

The Sacred Rock, is a monolith made from white granite, and stands 3 meters (10 feet) high, and rests on a 7 meter (23 feet) base. The rock is thought to represent the sacred animal puma, which is an Inca representation of earth. The rock is said to outline mountain Phutuq K'usi (Phutuqk'usi) behind it (some say also mountain Yanantin). The Sacred Rock is also seen as a gateway or portal between Machu Picchu and Mountain Huayna Picchu (seen in the left of the picture). The architecture of the plaza and rock strongly resembles that of the Sacred Plaza, by having two adjacent buildings with only three walls facing a central stone. The Sacred Rock is a powerful symbol in Machu Picchu, and seen as a spiritual area for meditation and absorbing positive energies.

Similar rocks called Wank'a, can be found throughout the region of Cusco. When the Spanish invaded Peru, they often used the Wank'a to build Catholic churches, such as the one at Qoyllority. The gate to climb mountain Huayna Picchu is directly to the left of the rock.

One of the buildings in front of the Sacred Rock. The bench is a modern additional to allow people to rest and mediate here.

Go behind the Sacred Rock and follow the path to the right. If you want to rest for a while first, take the path leading off to the right, else go left at the fork to see the rest of Machu Picchu.

Follow the rock path on the left to continue, or take a short break in the rest area (pictured below) to the right of the split.

The path forward is a bit rocky, so watch your step.

Just before you get to the lower Cemetery, there is an open area where you will have stunning views of mountain Huayna Picchu.

Mountain Huayna Picchu in the background.

From the open area, you can go down to the lower Cemetery by a small path that starts on the left just before you enter the open area. Once you are done viewing the lower Cemetery, come back up and then take the small path to the right between the buildings and then down the steps.

Lower Cemetery

The Lower Cemetery was named by Bingham, due to the cluster of burials he found there. Although there were other places that remains were found as well, the upper and lower cemetery held the most amount of burials per site. It is argued that due to there being two different cemetery sites, that there were two different classes at Machu Picchu. The lower cemetery was possibly used by the working class that lived in the buildings close by, while the upper cemetery were possibly used by priests. Note the large rock, in the distance, as seen in the next picture, no one knows what its purpose was.

Buildings behind the open area. Head towards the Sacred Plaza and then follow the path down to the left.

The Intiwatana will be across from you, go left.

Pictured next, follow the steps directly in front of you until you come to a T-junction at the bottom. To the left is the Temple of the Condor and the Mirror Pools, and to the right the Solar Tower, Pachamama's Cave (Royal Tomb), the Palace of the Princess, and the exit.

The Sun Pools / Mirror Pools / Industrial Area

After turning left at the bottom of the steps from the previous picture, you will have the view from the next picture. Go left into the rooms for the Mirror Pools (Mortars).

Harim Bingham called this section the Industrial Sector because of the two round pools, he found carved into rocks inside one room, as well as pottery and stone tools found here. Bingham thought that the rocks may have been used as mortars to grind corn, but it has not been proven. Some say the pools were used to watch the reflection of the sun and constellations and foresee the future. However, they fail to note that the building once had a roof.

Mortars. Note the pegs in the walls that were used to tie the roof down.

From the close-up, one can see that a lot of time and effort were spent in creating these two objects. Even the base was carved in a shape, especially the one on the left. Some say that this was to allow the workers to sit with their legs astride of the mortar while they grind corn. However, others say that if the pools were used to grind corn, it would have made more sense to make the base larger, or not bother in spending time to make a triangle base. This is one of the reasons some people think that the pools may have been used for scrying (divination).

Torture Chamber

From the Mirror pools, head out and then follow the path as seen in the following pictures. Do not go directly down to the Condor, first head over to the torture chambers. Bingham called the torture chamber and temple of the condor the prison group due to the buildings looking like a labyrinth, and from the appearance of the torture chamber.

Take the path to the right just behind the wall.

It is possible that prisoners were led down this path.

Bingham thought that the holes may have been used to bind prisoners while being tortured. Another theory is that the place may have been a temple where holy objects were stored. Priests may have used the flat surface to stand or sit on while praying. However, some combine Bingham's theory with the theory of a temple and say that it may have been used to bind people and sacrifice them. The flat surface allowed priests to stand on as well as collect the offered blood and channel it down to the condor temple below.

In the next picture, you can see how the blood would have flowed down into the sacred condor formation.

Anton Swanepoel

From this view, turn right and follow the path down and then to the left around the condor to its base.

Temple of the Condor

The temple of the condor is one of the more interesting objects at Machu Picchu. Unlike the mirror pools or the Intiwatana, the rock here was purposely carved to represent a condor. The head is formed by a stone in the ground, while the rock formation in the back forms the wings. There is a passage going into the rock formation, with a niche where offers are given. This is seen as a holy prayer area, as it is in the heart of the condor. The condor was also seen as a messenger of the gods, and this may have been a place where priests communicated with the gods via the condor.

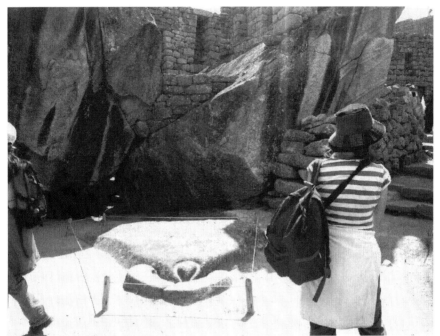

The rock formation at the back (torture chamber) forms the wings.

The head of the Condor.

Anton Swanepoel

A close-up of the rock formation forming the wings of the Condor.

After viewing the head of the condor, go through the tunnel between the wings to the prayer area, and then back out. From the next picture, one can see how big the condor is.

Follow the chamber below the Condor, it goes on a while, then does a 90 degree turn to the left where a shrine is located. Keep going on towards the exit and the royal residence that includes the Royal Tomb and Solar Temple. The emperor's residence is at the first fountain, ensuring he had the cleanest water.

Anton Swanepoel

When you leave the Condor, head towards the Royal Tomb and Solar Temple (the path that the people in the back of the picture are taking). Follow the steps up towards the Solar Tower next to the open building with the thatched roof in the middle of the photo. The bottom part houses the tomb, and just to the left of the tomb near the steps leading up to the Solar Towers is the Palace of the Princess.

Royal Tomb / Intimachay / Pachamama's Cave

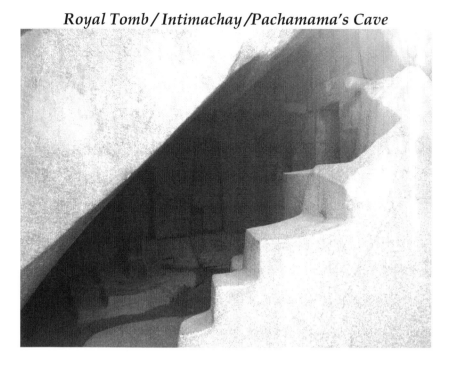

The Royal Tomb (Pachamama's Cave), is under the Solar Tower. It is believed to have housed offerings to the gods, or served as a tomb housing important mummies. The steps seen in front are thought to represent the underworld, earth, and heaven. There are faint engravings in the steps of the cave, which meaning has to date not been identified. A theory is that the remains of ancestral Inca emperors, possibly even Pachucuti after his death, was stored here.

Besides the Temple of the Sun is a two-story building known as the Palace of the Princess (Temple of Pachamama, also called the Nusta's Bedroom). Bingham gave the name to the building due to the beautiful walls and tall niches for offerings. The room may have been used by either the Princess or a high priest. No human remains were found in either the Royal Tomb or the Palace of the Princess. Many believe that it was used to give offering to the earth mother or the moon, Pachamama. The Incas believed their ancestors where the sun and the moon. Interestingly, only during sunrise of the 10 days before and after the summer solstice (21 December), does the light reach the back wall of the cave.

Temple of the Sun / Torreon / Solar Tower

The Solar Tower. Picture by Catalina Villamil

The Temple of the Sun is located next to the first fountain and also the Royal House. The temple's foundation is a massive white, granite boulder, while the palace walls follow the curve of the bedrock. Some scholars believe that the temple was used as an astronomical observatory to track the sun's path, as well as keep a calendar. This is due to the fact that on the winter solstice (21 June), the morning sun's rays pass through a small opening and lines up with the bedrock inside. The tower has several niches that may have been used to hold offerings to the sun god.

It should be noted that the Temple of the Sun at Machu Picchu is not the only one, as well as it is actually small compared to others. A number of other Sun Temples have been found at other locations, including at the ruins of Pisac that also has residential and royal quarters, as well as a Sun Temple similar to Machu Picchu.

The main Sun Temple is in Cusco. This temple was hidden in the walls of a Dominican priory. In 1950, a severe earthquake shook Peru and did massive damage to the priory, revealing the inner walls of the hidden temple. On excavating the temple, it was found that it was dedicated to the sun, moon, rainbow, and lightning. Massive niches are in the temple, and thought to have once housed the mummies of the past Peruvian rules and their consorts. The mummies are believed to have been removed when the Spanish invaded Peru, and that they may have been buried in the Urubamba valley. In the valley, a site was found where the ground forms a temple in perspective due to lines running through the ground, when viewed from a nearby mountain. On the day of the winter solstice, the first morning light shines through the valley and illuminates a gate at the edge of the valley. It is though that this may lead to the resting place of the mummies.

It is interesting to note that a legend existed in the Inca times that a race of unknown origin will arrive and destroy their empire. It is believed that if the Inca emperor did not die, causing the empire to split, they would have crushed the Spanish invaders. In addition, the Incas were only about 100,000 people, and ruled harshly over around 10 to 12 million people. Many saw the invading Spanish as a lesser evil than the Incas that demanded tributes, which included the sacrifice of noble children.

From the Solar Temple, you can follow this path up back to the rest of the ruins. If you turn left at the top you can go to the Inca Bridge and the big mountain, Mount Machu Picchu. The exit is at the bottom of the steps and to the left, past the Royal Tomb and over the Dirt Ditch, as seen in the next picture.

Follow this path to the exit, you will come out just below the path you started the tour. There is a storeroom (granary) near the exit as you go up the path. The room is basic and consists of a large well ventilated, thatched room. The design is perfect as the room is far cooler than the surrounding temperature.

Dry Mount (Dirt Ditch)

The dirt ditch was the main drainage of rain water for Machu Picchu. Most of the water from the 130 drains emptied into the Sacred Square, from there it was channeled underground towards the ditch. Without this design, landslides would have occurred and Machu Picchu would have slid off the mountain long ago.

Chapter 7: Inca Bridge

To get to the Inca Bridge, pass by the Guard House and then go over a small bridge. Keep going past the Barracks and Upper Cemetery. The path is not as scary as climbing either mountain, but it is no picnic either as can be seen in the following pictures.

Pictured above, the guard station to sign in and out. At times, waiting to sign in or out takes longer than walking to the actual bridge. The path itself is relatively easy to follow and takes around 30 minutes.

It is amazing how they build a path right up the mountain.

Part of the path goes over some larger rocks, so watch your step.

Soon you will pass through some rocks and see the bridge, in the distance, against the rock face. The bridge is now closed to tourist due to safety concerns. If Machu Picchu was attacked, the wooden planks over the gap could be pulled away, stopping enemy warriors from using the path. Up to the last few meters, the path should be not too bad for people suffering from vertigo or fear of heights. However, the last part is around a large boulder with a very narrow path and a sheer drop-off. There is a cable to hang onto while you negotiate the last section, do use the cable.

The last bit to the bridge, do use the cable. If you did either mountain, you will find this not really scary.

A wooden gate blocks you from going any further, just in case you had the inclination of actually walking the planks. Even if enemy warriors did manage to cross the bridge, they would only be able to cross in single file and would be bottled up by this narrow passage that could easily be defended by throwing rocks down.

Chapter 8: Mountain Huayna Picchu

Pictured above is the entrance to the path leading to Mountain Huayna Picchu. The entry is behind the Sacred Rock. The gate opens at 7am, and there are two scheduled passed, 7am, and 9am. If your ticket says 9am, the guard will not allow you to pass before 9am. Note that the gate closes at 1pm.

Important, without a ticket to the mountain, which can only be purchased when you purchase your ticket for Machu Picchu, you cannot climb the mountain. Only 400 tickets are sold a day, so book early if you plan on climbing the mountain.

Mountain Huayna Picchu is far more popular and easier to climb than Mountain Machu Picchu. The climb is around 45 minutes to an hour one way. At some points, the path can be a bit scary for those who do not like heights. However, there are wooden railings and metal cables installed to calm your heart. A little way down from the start of the path you will find a split in the road. To the left is the peak Huchy Picchu, and to the right is Mountain Huayna Picchu, as well as the Lunar Temple and Grand Cavern. To my knowledge, the path to Huchy Picchu goes over the peak and links up with the main path again.

The view is amazing. Below, one can see how far the terraces stretch that brace the mountain. Mountain Huayna Picchu is one side of the ridgeline when the section the ruins are on, sank in. Far below one can see the sacred Urubamba River. The engineers of Machu Picchu kept in mind that the land was (and still is) heavily prone to earthquakes. They used a technique called ashlar, whereby they fitted stone blocks together without using mortar. This allows individual stones to move during an earthquake and settle back into their original places without damage to the building.

Pictured above, the trail goes up and down, although there are more ups than downs. This path actually is part of the over 16,000 kilometer (almost 10, 000 miles) network of roads that the Incas built.

Up and up the trail goes, nice exercise for your leg muscle. Do watch your step, especially if it has rained.

The path at places switchbacks across the mountain, but is not that difficult if you are reasonably fit. Just take it slow and drink plenty of water.

Some of the steps can be small with no railing, go on all fours if you need to, but just do not fall backwards or slip. You may want to think about bringing thin garden gloves to protect your hands.

Note the cable to help you climb up the path, use it, no hero stuff.

Just before you reach the top, there is an open area where you can pose for a photo. Trying to smile while you are huffing and puffing is another thing though. ☺ In the back is the ruins, one can see the road that the buses use to transport people to Machu Picchu. If you decide to not take a bus but to rather hike up to Machu Picchu, take note that that is what you will need to climb to get to the gate.

Pictured next: to get to the top, you need to go through an opening that some call small, clearly they have not been cave diving. ☺ If you have a backpack on, take it off and push it in front of you to stop you from damaging it and to make passing through easier.

Some say that this passage resembles that of a woman's womb and that Machu Picchu was a spiritual destination after a spiritual journey, and that this signifies being reborn as you exit the passage. On top, the view is similar to seeing everything in life clearly as to seeing the bigger picture.

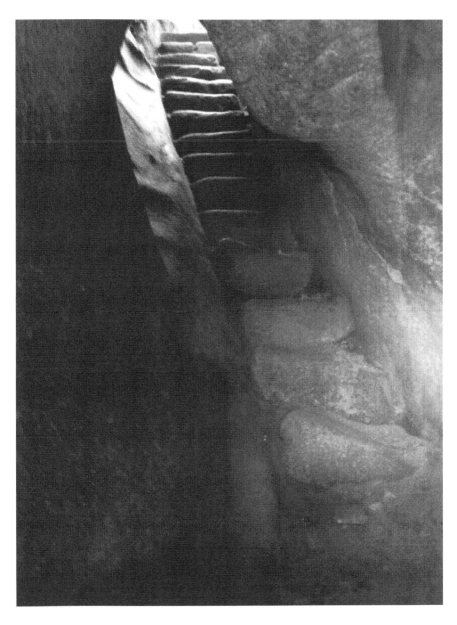

After passing through the opening in the rock you will be on the top. There are a few rocks where you can sit, just watch your step. Those that do not like heights may want to let this one pass.

Looking down while sitting on one of the rocks.

Make sure you have boots that grip and a good seating.

The Incas worshiped the sun, earth, and water the same way. Machu Picchu is a testament to this, as they brought the three elements together in a magnificent feat. In Inca times, it was a five-day walk from Cusco to Machu Picchu, and visitors would pass through the Intipunki (Doorway of the Sun), past the Guard House and through the Inca Doorway into Machu Picchu.

The path to the caves is down and to the right. To return without going to the caves go left. I just slid down where the big rock is but I do not suggest this. There are easier ways down.

The space is limited here, as only 400 people are allowed to climb this per day, I would recommend you climb the mountain first, then go and see the ruins. Most tourists arrive around 10am, so from 11am on the mountain gets packed. I also recommend some cheap gloves. There are times when you will be dragging yourself up by old rusty cables or rocks. The cables do not have splinters, but the rust gives off on your hands.

The top of Mountain Huayna Picchu is 2,720 meters (8924 feet) above sea level, and stands 370 meters (1214 feet) above Machu Picchu.

View from the top of Huayna Picchu. Image from fotolia.

You can go on to the Grand Cavern and the Lunar Temple or return from here. The sign in the back says 'Continue' and is if you want to return. Behind you is the path to the Grand Cavern.

Chapter 9: Lunar Temple and Grand Cavern

To get to either the Lunar Temple or the Grand Cavern, follow the start of the path as shown before, and down the section pictured next. It will add about 1½ to two hours additional to your trip, making the total trip roughly four hours.

The path is marked with arrows and easy to follow.

The path itself is relatively easy and has guide cables in some places.

Still going down, now getting more rain forest like.

There is a 30 foot drop with a wooden ladder – good thing there are no termites here. It really is not scary, and if you are afraid of heights, just look at the ladder post in front of you and slowly go down one step at a time. This is probably the scariest bit of the path (until the return at the back of the mountain). ☺

Gloves come in handy.

Anton Swanepoel

Soon you will come to a doorway. The path leads down to the right and passes through the doorway under me. To the left of the photo, above my head height, is an open area where some people sit to pray. The Lunar Temple is on the left after passing through the doorway, and the Grand Cavern is to the right further down. The Grand Cavern is 454 meters (1,489 feet) below the summit of Mountain Huayna Picchu, at a height of 2266 meters (7434 feet) above sea level, on the north side. Mummies have been found in the caverns, and it is believed that the area was used as a sacred ceremonial site. The stonework here is some of the best of Machu Picchu, and is said to contain the three planes of the Incan religion, being: the Hanan Pacha (the heavens, condor), the Kay Pacha (the earth, puma), and the Ukju Pacha (the underworld, snakes).

The name of the site is under despite, as some say it was used to worship the moon and is due to how the moon enters the cave at night. However, no evidence has been found linking the lunar cycle to the cave or shrines.

A closer look at the doorway, pass through it to get to the Lunar Temple and to return to Machu Picchu (left); as well as the Grand Cavern (right and further down).

Left view of the Lunar Temple. The Lunar astral rock is just to the right of the photo.

Looking to the right, we see the large rock that has a hollowed out portion that you can sit in and have a rest, or use it to pray in.

Behind the astral rock is a small cavern. There are some areas that local people and others use to pray and leave offerings.

Pictured above, the last part of the Lunar Temple, is still actively used by people to leave offerings and pray.

Looking out of the Lunar Temple, the astral rock directly in front.

Looking a bit to the right, still in the temple, we note a flat surface on a large rock in front of us, interesting how it was created, as too the whole Temple.

View from the astral rock, the Grand Cavern is down to the right.

Entrance to the Grand Cavern.

Structure on top of the Cavern.

Looking up towards the Lunar Temple.

Stepped back view of the Cavern.

Cavern entrance.

Anton Swanepoel

There are a number of shrine like openings inside with rocks in them.

In one large area, a rock is situated on a larger flat rock and is clearly still being used to grind stuff. The Cavern is still actively used by many to pray and leave offerings.

To return to Machu Picchu, go back up to the Lunar Temple and pass right by it, following the sign to Machu Picchu. Pictured above, the start of the path back. You have to climb all that you descended back up again.

Anton Swanepoel

Slowly going up, the surroundings are very beautiful.

Some of the path cuts through rain forest like surroundings.

More steps, going up and up.

Stunning views on your way back, all worth the effort.

Anton Swanepoel

Up and up we go.

On your way back, you will pass by some ruins.

Anton Swanepoel

The path back goes around the ruins and then down, stunning views.

From here we can see Machu Picchu in the distance. The path goes down and then up over the peak in front.

At times the path gets a bit steep.

Anton Swanepoel

Some of the path goes around the rock face and has only a small edge to help you not to fall off, be careful and take it easy.

And now we start to climb up again; it is a workout. And to think my hotel has a gym in it, why on earth would you want a gym session after this? ☺

Very nice surroundings as you slug it back up all those stairs. Remember to rest every now and again, and drink plenty of water.

Some of the path passes under a rock, very interesting how it was cut out.

Anton Swanepoel

Oh, and yes, you have to climb a ladder again, but this one is very small. Soon after this, you will be on the path that you came down and where the split in the path was that you could either go to the mountain or the Lunar Temple.

Looking back at the path you just came from on the left, the right path leads to the mountain. If you came to this point at the start of your trip and did not want to go to the top of the mountain but just to the caves, turn left here. However, I recommend climbing to the top, it is well worth it.

Almost there, just a bit more.

Chapter 10: Mountain Machu Picchu

Mountain Machu Picchu is on the far southern side of the complex, towards the Inti Punku. From just below the Guard House follow this path to reach the entrance gate. The small path leading left and up in the middle of the photo where the people are, is the path to climb Mountain Machu Picchu.

Know that Lamas have the right of way, but are harmless. Do get a Lama hair jersey and socks in the town below, they are awesomely warm and soft.

Pictured above is the entrance to the path leading to Mountain Machu Picchu. The gate opens at 7am, and you are allowed to start climbing the mountain until 11am. You have to be back by 2pm (14h00). Only 300 people are allowed to climb the mountain each day, and the climb up will take around 1 ½ to two hours. This mountain is far harder and scarier to climb than Mountain Huayan Picchu, but offers breathtaking views. Not all who start the climb finish it, as many mistake this for the 45-minute climb, mountain Huayna Picchu, and greatly underestimates this mountain. When I climbed the mountain, I was number 14 to sign in, but number 10 on the mountain. When I returned to the gate just after 11am, it was closed for starting the climb, I noted 181 people had signed in. However, only around 15 people had passed me, making a possible 26 people or so that reached the top that day. The rest had turned around. Do make sure you allow enough time to do the climb. It is about a four-hour round trip.

Note that you need an access ticket to climb the mountain. This is purchased as an add-on to your Machu Picchu ticket.

After what feels like climbing half the mountain, you eventually come to the access control gate. Remember to have your passport here and entry ticket, with plenty of water. Take it slow when climbing, and take frequent rest and water breaks. The top of the mountain towers 730 meters (around 2,395 feet) above Machu Picchu (Intiwatana), at an altitude of around 3080 meters (10105 feet). It is said that there are over 2000 steps to the top.

Some of the steps can be small and the rocks loose, watch your step. It is advised to wear some garden gloves or light mechanic gloves as you may be doing some of the path on all fours.

Still easy going and awesome views.

Anton Swanepoel

Looking back down the path. In many places, the path is totally open and there are no ropes or railings on any part of the path. If you do not like heights, then just take it one-step at a time and look down at the steps and keep going, you will be greatly rewarded when you come to the top.

Along the way, you will pass by some small ruins.

Stunning view as you climb up.

Picture from freeimages.

Keep going, not too far now.

Anton Swanepoel

Looking back the way you came. Do not slip and fall.

The path cuts between some rocks and then goes around to the right.

Anton Swanepoel

The other side of passing between the rocks.

Almost there, the hut-like structure in the background is the top of the mountain.

Last steps to the top, well done.

Although the area here is larger than Mountain Huayna Picchu, still watch your step. At the top of the mountain, there is a little shaded area where you can rest, but not much else. The view is what it is all about.

Looking back the way you came, hard work.

The end of the mountain, here you look down onto Machu Picchu and the river.

Anton Swanepoel

Looking back at the hut.

Machu Picchu in the distance below, clouds passing by.

Side of the mountain, Inca trail faintly visible in the bottom right of the photo. Clouds coming over the tops of the surrounding mountains.

You are surrounded by Sacred Mountains.

Stunning view of the Urubamba River below.

Looking back to the end of the top where the path comes up. The path up to the mountain drops down to the right of the photo at the end just by the rounding of the flat bit.

Anton Swanepoel

Chapter 11: Intipunku / The Door of The Sun

To get to the Inti Punku, use the same path as if going to Mountain Machu Picchu, and just keep going. The path is not as hard or scary as climbing either mountain, but it is a bit long, taking around 1½ hours on a comfortable hike.

Pictured above, the path zigzags along the mountain, in the middle, the cross lines in the photo are the path, and way in the back, the small black spots are the ruins of Inti Punku.

Note, if you took the Inca trail, this is one of the paths you will use to enter Machu Picchu. Pictured next, on your way to Inti Punku, you will pass some prayer grounds where people pile rocks and say prayers. All the little piles of stones are prayers, directed at the sacred rock in the background of the first picture. This part of Machu Picchu is not as crowded, and you are likely to find a number of people that use the area for spiritual enlightenment. Expect to see people praying and listening to spiritual mentors.

A little while into your hike, you will pass some ruins and a very interesting rock.

View towards Machu Picchu from Inti Punku.

The Inti Punku is one of the doorways or gates to Machu Picchu. It is believed that this may have been both a military checkpoint, as well as a ritual site. Due to the sun rising behind the mountains, it would be around 10am in the morning before the sun shines directly onto Machu Picchu. Except for Mountain Machu Picchu, this is the only place you can see the sunrise over Machu Picchu.

Chapter 12: Hot Springs

The hot springs is a short walk from the plaza in Machu Picchu Pueblo. The springs are seen as highly spiritual and to promote healing, due to the strong mineral (sulfur) found in the water. The water is naturally warm and often used as medical therapy, especially for rheumatism. The warm water also helps to rid one of stress and toxins, while enhancing your metabolism.

The hot springs is normally open from 8am to 5pm, although in some months when the sun sets later, it is sometimes open at different times. Check operating hours when you enter. You can rent towels and bathing costumes outside the gate for around 10 Sol.

From this view, take the small path to the right that leads up, after passing over the bridge.

Anton Swanepoel

The path winds all along the river for most of the part. Turn left and go through a small plaza when this path ends at a large rock. Continue past a few shops and through the entry gate, then on until the path ends at a small restaurant by the hot springs.

Go through the plaza to the back and then turn right.

Anton Swanepoel

You can purchase some snacks and rent a bathing costume and a towel from the shops just before you come to the entry gate.

After purchasing your ticket at the gate, continue up towards the hot springs. (Note, the view is looking down at the road you just came up to get to the springs. At the shops in the background you can rent towels and bathing costumes. The hot springs is behind the view.)

Pictured next, the path up to the hot springs is very well maintained and has some good views. As you go up, you will notice to the right of the river the remains of the original hot springs that got damaged in the last floods of January 2010.

Pass through the restaurant to get to the hot springs.

Anton Swanepoel

The area has a bar and some comfy chairs to relax in.

The stairs that you will come from after the changing rooms are in the far back left of the photo.

Anton Swanepoel

There is a storage area where you can leave stuff if needed. The first pool was ice cold. The second one recorded 38 degrees Celsius (101 degrees Fahrenheit) on my dive computer. The next one was a bit cooler at 35 degrees Celsius (95 degrees Fahrenheit). In the summer, the temperatures may go up to 45 degrees Celsius (113 degrees Fahrenheit)

There are showers at the bottom of the pools that some locals use to wash themselves. The bottoms of the pools are filled with small pebbles, and the water is said to contain sulfur that is thought to help in treating ailments such as rheumatism, stress, and high blood pressure, in addition to getting rid of toxins and aiding metabolism.

Chapter 13: Helpful Websites

This is a list of websites that can help you both in planning your trip and giving you more information about Peru and Machu Picchu. Some of the websites listed here are listed elsewhere in the book, while some are not.

USA State Department website about Peru
http://travel.state.gov/content/passports/english/country.html
http://travel.state.gov/content/passports/english/country/peru.html

Bus information
www.cusco-peru.info/cusco_buses.htm

Portable applications running from a USB flash drive
http://portableapps.com/

Information about Machu Picchu
www.lonelyplanet.com/peru/machu-picchu
www.go2peru.com/ecs_ing.htm
http://www.visitperu.com/
www.machupicchuperu.info
http://www.imachupicchu.com/

Information about Lima
www.limaeasy.com/index.php

Tickets to Machu Picchu
www.ticket-machupicchu.com
www.machupicchu.gob.pe (government website)

Booking Accommodations
www.bookings.com
www.expedia.com
http://www.interhabit.com/

Train Tickets

www.perurail.com
www.incarail.com
www.machupicchutrain.com
www.peru-machu-picchu.com/index.php
www.orient-express.com/web/hb/hiram_bingham.jsp
www.ferrocarrilcentral.com.pe/index_.php

Travel Agents

www.cusco-peru.info/eng/index_eng.html
www.perutreks.com/index.html
www.peruforless.com
www.andeantravelweb.com/peru/index.html
www.llamaexpeditions.com
www.trails.com/machu-picchu.html
www.machupicchutickets.com

Visas

http://www.limaeasy.com/peru-info/peruvian-visa
http://www.embaperu.org.au/embassy/visas.html

Weather

www.accuweather.com/en/pe/machu-picchu/262837/weather-forecast/262837
www.worldweatheronline.com/v2/weather.aspx?q=MFT
www.zoover.co.uk/peru/peru/machu-picchu/weather
www.intermeteo.com/south_america/peru/machu_picchu

Stopping Google from reverting to local language

www.google.com/ncr

Maps

www.rediscovermachupicchu.com/mp-maps.htm

Chapter 14: Maps

This chapter includes maps for the main roads you will use in Ollantaytambo, Machu Picchu Pueblo, and the Machu Picchu ruins. There is also a high level map showing the location of the towns towards the ruins, such as Lima and Cusco. This will help you get an orientation of Peru.

Note, these are maps on third party websites out of my control and may go down without notice.

For more detailed and printable maps of Machu Picchu go to *http://www.rediscovermachupicchu.com/mp-maps.htm*

See the links to specific maps on the page, or follow these links:

Machu Picchu Area Map
http://www.interhabit.com/ Use the interactive map search.

Machu Picchu Internal Layout Maps
http://www.go2peru.com/destinos/large/map_incatrail_ing.jpg
http://leegilchrist.net/images/Peru/Machu%20Picchu/Machu%20Picchu%20map%202.jpg
http://moon.com/maps/south-america/peru/
http://static.moon.com/wp-content/uploads/2013/05/peru_01_Machu-Picchu.jpg

Aguas-Calientes
http://static.moon.com/wp-content/uploads/2013/05/peru_01_Aguas-Calientes.jpg

Ollanaytamo-City
http://static.moon.com/wp-content/uploads/2013/05/peru_01_Ollanaytamo-City.jpg

Inca Trail to Machu Picchu Maps

http://www.inkaterra.com/images/maps/machu-picchu-map-01.jpg
http://www.go2peru.com/destinos/large/map_incatrail_ing.jpg

Machu Picchu Pueblo

http://www.imachupicchu.com/

Lima

http://static.moon.com/wp-content/uploads/2013/05/peru_05_Lima.jpg
http://static.moon.com/wp-content/uploads/2013/05/peru_05_Central-Lima.jpg

Cusco

http://static.moon.com/wp-content/uploads/2013/05/peru_01_Cusco-City.jpg
http://static.moon.com/wp-content/uploads/2013/05/peru_01_Cusco-and-the-Sacred-Valley.jpg

Maps of Machu Picchu

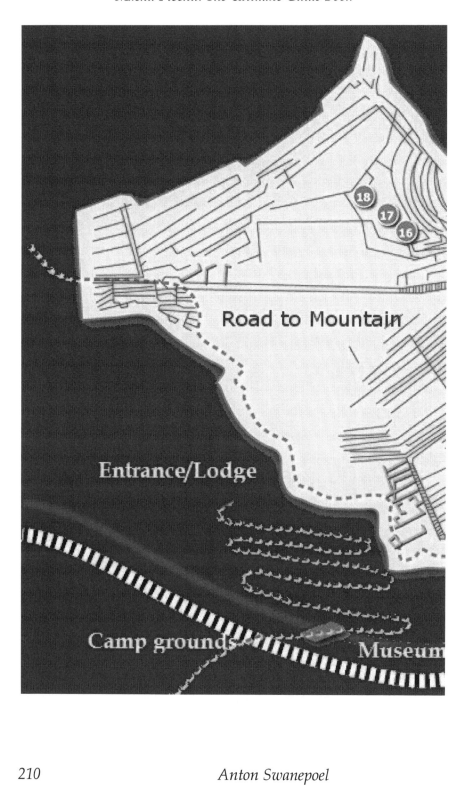

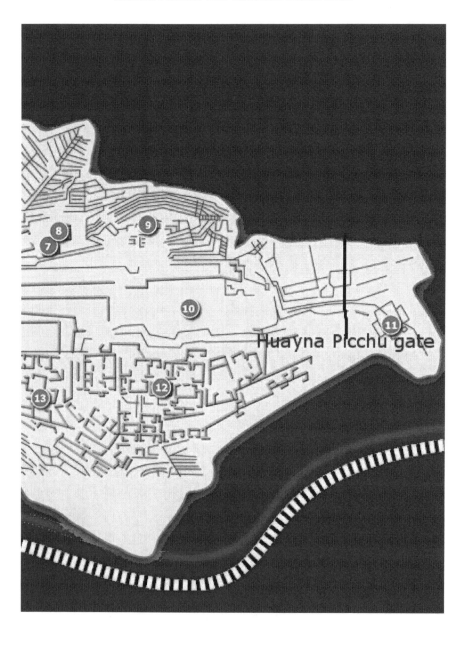

Anton Swanepoel

1: City Gate
2: Nusta's bedroom
3: Temple of the Sun
4: Royal Tomb
5: Ritual Fountains
Mirror Pools
6: Royal Palace
7: Temple of 3 Windows
8: Main Temple
9: Intiwatana

10: Main square
11: Sacred Rock/ Huayna Picchu
12: House of Factories
13: Industrial Zone
14: Prisoner's area / Condor Temple /

15: Cultivation Zone
16: House of the Guardians
17: Funeral Rock /Guard House
18: Cemetery

When you enter the ruins, you can take the long way that will first lead you to the road to the Mountain Machu Picchu and the Funeral Rock (17) and Guard House. You can then proceed down to the main entrance (1) to the ruins themselves. From there go to the Temple of the Three Windows (7) and up to Intiwatana (9). The path will now take you down to the Sacred Rock / entrance to Mountain Huayna Picchu (11). You can now work your way around on the other side of the main square (10) towards the House of Factories /Mirror Pools (12) and from there to the prisoner's area/ Temple of the Condor (14). From here you can go up towards the Temple of the Sun (3) and Nusta's bedroom (Palace of the Princess) (2).

Map of Machu Picchu Pueblo
First photo rotated 90 degrees to the right to enhance size

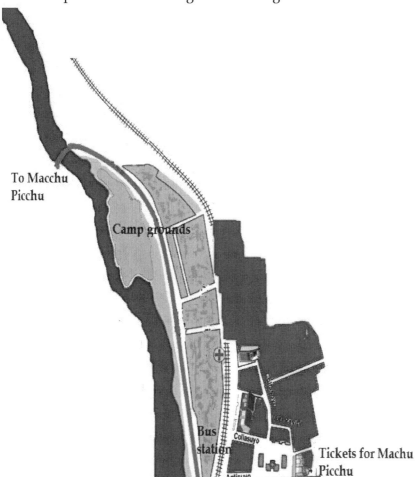

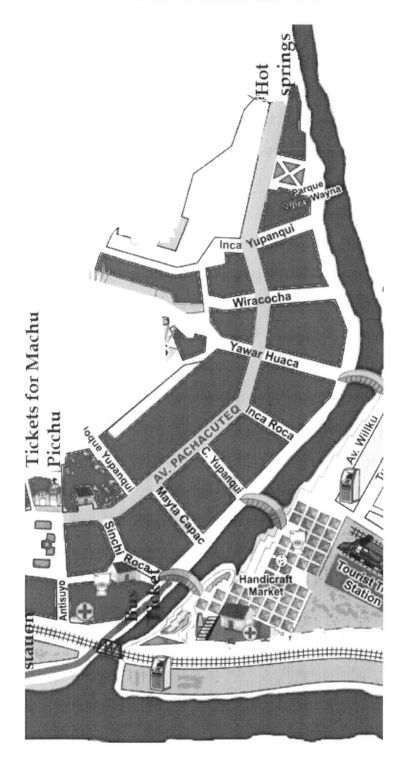

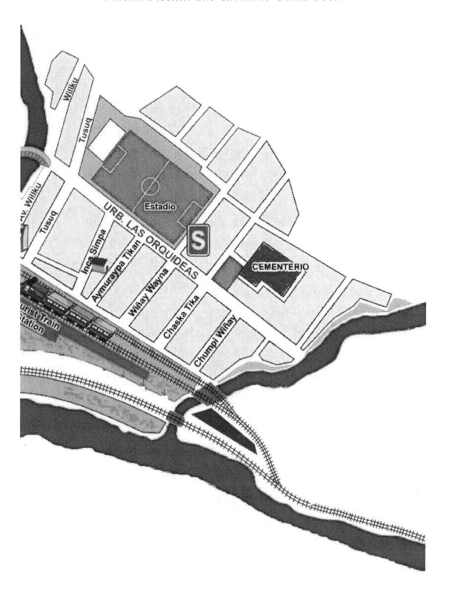

Thank you for taking the time to read *Machu Picchu: The Ultimate Guide to Exploring Machu Picchu and its Hidden Attractions.*

If you enjoyed this book or found it useful, I would be very grateful if you would please post a short review because your support really does make a difference. Alternatively, consider telling your friends about this book because word of mouth is an author's best friend and much appreciated.

Thank you very much for your time.

Anton Swanepoel

If you want to contact me personally, send me an email @ *anton@antonswanepoelbooks.com*

Follow this link if you want updates on new book releases by me, as well as travel tips from my blog posts.
http://antonswanepoelbooks.com/subscribe.php

About the Author

Anton Swanepoel @ Pol Pot's house on the mountains in Thailand, and on his way to Preah Vihear Temple.

For seven years, I worked as a technical diving instructor in the Cayman Islands. I am a Tri-Mix instructor in multiple agencies, and dove to over 400ft on open circuit. While on Grand Cayman, I started a passion that I always had, writing. For a number of years, I saved what I could, and in Jan 2014, I moved to Siem Reap, Cambodia, to focus full-time on my writing, while travelling. If you want to follow my adventures, see my blog www.antonswanepoelbooks.com/blog.

Anton Swanepoel

More Books by Anton

Novels
Laura and The Jaguar Prophecy (Book 1)
Laura and The God Code (Book 2)

Travel Diary
Almost Somewhere

Peru Travel
Machu Picchu: The Ultimate Guide to Machu Picchu

Travel Tips
Angkor Wat & Cambodia
100 International Travel Tips
Backpacking SouthEast Asia

Motorbike Travel
Motorcycle: A Guide Book To Long Distance And Adventure Riding
Motorbiking Cambodia & Vietnam

Cambodia Travel
Cambodia: 50 Facts You Should Know When Visiting Cambodia
Angkor Wat: 20 Must See Temples
Angkor Wat Temples
Angkor Wat Archaeological Park
Kampot, Kep and Sihanoukville
Kampot: 20 Must See Attractions
Kep: 10 Must See Attractions
Sihanoukville: 20 Must See Attractions
Battambang: 20 Must See Attractions
Phnom Penh: 20 Must See Attractions
Siem Reap: 20 Must See Attractions
Dangerous Loads

Vietnam Travel
Vietnam: 50 Facts You Should Know When Visiting Vietnam
Vietnam Caves
Ha Long Bay
The Perfumed Pagoda
Phong Nha Caves

Thailand
Thailand: 50 Facts You Should Know When Visiting Thailand
Bangkok: 20 Must See Attractions
Ayutthaya: 20 Must See Attractions
The Great Buddha

Laos
Vientiane: 20 Must See Attractions

South Africa
South Africa: 50 Facts You Should Know When Visiting South Africa
Pretoria: 20 Must See Attractions
Freedom Park
Union Buildings
The Voortekker Monument Heritage Site
The Cradle of Humankind Heritage Site

Diving Books
The Art of Gas Blending
Dive Computers
Gas Blender Program
Deep and Safety Stops, and Gradient Factors
Diving Below 130 Feet

Writing Books
Supercharge Your Book Description

Self Help Books
Ear Pain
Sea and Motion Sickness

Printed in Great Britain
by Amazon